The Beatles
or the
'White Album'

Edited by

Mark Goodall

HEADPRESS

Contents

IV   THE BEATLES, or the 'White Album'

Introduction

MARK GOODALL

This book on *The Beatles* LP (aka the 'White Album', released on Friday 22nd November 1968) was written during the commemorations of *Sgt. Pepper's Lonely Hearts Club Band*, the 'White Album's gaudy and somewhat overrated predecessor.

Critical opinion on *The Beatles* in 1968 was muted, the record being seen as something of a comedown after the exhilaration of the group's declared psychedelic masterpiece. Conventional wisdom holds that *The Beatles* marks the beginning of the end of the Lennon/McCartney partnership, as on this LP, the group, according to Roy Carr 'each act as each others' session men'[1]. *The Beatles* is thus seen to augur the start of the solo careers of the respective members of the group with a significant number of the tracks featuring one or two group members only, setting a precedent for the individualism to come soon after. Despite such issues, this book exists to argue that *The Beatles* is not only the finest achievement of the Beatles but can also be considered one of the greatest LP recordings of all time.

This book is not to be read as a scholarly study of *The Beatles* LP but rather as an experience like listening to the actual record itself: uneven, disorientating, difficult, entertaining. The contributions to the book, produced through a variety of modes of expression, reflect this wide-ranging approach where no two songs are the same. The Beatles, especially their managers, had done a good job of thus far presenting the group as a tight unit with extremely high standards of composition, musicianship and production. It is therefore the 'messiness' of *The Beatles* LP that is considered problematic, most famously by producer George Martin who wanted to edit the songs into a single LP. Unlike the relatively consistent style the previous LPs had offered, *The Beatles* revels in confusion. Is the LP rock'n'roll? Folk? Avant-garde? Rock? I would suggest that fifty years later such aesthetic 'confusion' demands a more thoughtful approach.

1 Carr, R and Tyler, T. *The Beatles: an Illustrated Record*. Little, Brown, 1998, p.74

Richard Alpert, who in the mid 1960s with Timothy Leary and Ralph Metzner, advocated use of mind-expanding hallucinogenic drugs, suggests one method of understanding *The Beatles*. In his book *Remember, Be Here Now*[1], Alpert talks about a 'journey' as being made up of three stages: 1) the social science stage; 2) the psychedelic stage and 3) the Yogi stage. Each stage follows and develops out of the other. To me, the Beatles career has progressed in such a manner. They began as a pop group expertly documenting love and teenage anguish before discovering existentialism, mind-expanding drugs and a questioning, psychedelic consciousness. *The Beatles* LP therefore can be viewed as representing the group's 'Yogic' phase — a disenchantment with the material success and adoration presented by the entertainment industry coupled with a desire to break fee of social and political norms. Stripped down to a basic instrumentation of acoustic guitars, the period the group spent under the guidance of Maharishi Mahesh Yogi created a new sense of reflection, introspection and revolution. This makes for an uneasy listening experience but over time, a rich and rewarding one.

This spiritual and thematic transformation went alongside a level of technical experimentation harnessing the latest radical developments in studio trickery. Engineer Stuart Epps (Elton John, Chris Rea) commented, on hearing a preview copy of the LP, that: 'It wasn't just like listening to new songs, it was listening to new technology'[2]. Radical times demanded radical creative responses. As any great artist knows 'every once in a while you have to change your material to keep the interest of your fans'[3]. George Harrison himself described the LP as 'Heavy to listen to'.

The Beatles was a break with the continuum of Beatles recordings; however, links still exist between their early phase and this later one. For example, the method of starting an LP recording with an exciting, upbeat track began on the first Beatles LP *Please Please Me* with I Saw Her Standing There. Similarly, *The Beatles* opens with a powerful rocker Back In The U.S.S.R. However, back in 1963 the group sang about raw, primal, sexual emotions. By 1968 this blueprint had become parodic, ironic and topical.

In producing this book it was clear that a textual approach to a musical work was in danger of reinforcing the famous statement

1 Alpert, A. *Remember, Be Here Now*. Lama Foundation, 1971, p.1

2 Cunningham, M. *Good Vibrations: a History of Record Production*, Castle 1996, p.143
3 Del Shannon quoted in Richard Meltzer. *The Aesthetics of Rock*. Da Capo, 1970, p.90

(attributed variously) that 'writing about music is as illogical as singing about economics'. As Richard Meltzer points out: 'when one talks about music its power is lessened, it loses its effectiveness'[1]. Despite this 'Rock is a totality: it contains or implies that it can contain, all varieties of experience'[2] and *The Beatles*, with its genuinely kaleidoscopic mix of musical forms, stands as a prime example of this idea.

The period following the release of *The Beatles* LP is viewed as an attempt by the group returning to its roots, getting 'back to basics'. The project designed to do this was of course the *Let It Be* record and documentary film. In fact, this process began with *The Beatles*. Both works display the reality of the group's creative and working practices. *The Beatles* offers, in place of the fantasy notion that previous records were made by a coherent and unchanging unit, a deconstruction of the recording process: scraps of unfinished tunes; improvisation; sequencing; collage. It's the first glimpse of the Beatles 'unplugged'. In *Let It Be* we experience the Beatles jamming, rehearsing, developing individual songs. We can see the seemingly magic transformation of rough, demo versions of a song into a finished work (Two of

Us, for example)[3]. The transmutation of base elements of musical expression becomes as magical as any psychedelic trip.

The iconic nature of *The Beatles* has not been lost on other creative groups and individuals, its white, or off-white, easily stained visage becoming as striking in its own way as the baroque pop art excesses of *Sgt. Pepper's Lonely Hearts Club Band*. Due to the high number of takes of the songs on the recording (in some ways it is *The Beatles* that made the most extensive use of the recording studio and not its predecessor) bootleg copies of the LP quickly surfaced in a number of manifestations of varying technical quality and coloured vinyl hue. The demo tapes for the LP, recorded by George Harrison at his house 'Kinfauns', also become the subject of furious bootlegging and repackaging with the 'Esher Demos' becoming almost as famous as the original LP.

A collection of recordings by deranged Beatles fan Charles Manson was issued by the Grey Matter label in 1993 and mimics the 'White Album' packaging — the faces of Manson and his followers replacing those of the Fab Four. In the same year San Francis-

1 Meltzer, p.245
2 Ibid.

3 This effect also occurs in the Jean-Luc Godard film *Sympathy for the Devil* (*One Plus One*, 1968), where the Rolling Stones are seen recording Sympathy For The Devil.

can outfit Big City Orchestra released a CD entitled *Beatlerape* a distorted noise package of experimental abstract Beatles cover versions. In 2004 Brian Joseph Burton, aka Danger Mouse, issued *The Grey Album*, a mash-up of *The Beatles* and rapper Jay-Z's *The Black Album*. To mark the fortieth anniversary of the LP release the British music magazine *Mojo* issued a CD of cover versions of the songs on the record. The variety of responses (good and bad… mostly bad) is indicative of how open and free the spirit of the original LP continues to be well into the twentieth century.

Perhaps the most interesting project was the one created by American artist Rutherford Chang. *The 'White Album'* was created by sonically layering one hundred unique copies of *The Beatles* LP. Chang's project 'captures how every copy of the iconic album has been distinctly shaped by its history, both visually and sonically. The forty-five-year-old albums, with scratches and physical imperfections accumulated with age, all play slightly differently, causing the 100 layers to gradually drift out of sync over the course of each side.'[1] In a marker of its defiant nature, Chang's recording has been removed from the record collecting website Discogs (see Fig.1).

Chang's associated 'We Buy White Albums' project is made from an on-going collection of over 1,800 numbered pressings of *The Beatles* that the artist has collected. Each copy of the LP is in different state of decay. The most interesting copies, from a conceptual point of view, are the ones that, due to water or heat damage, barely resemble the original vinyl LP or have been modified by their owners in show way (some people have coloured in the embossed 'BEATLES' lettering; one copy bizarrely has the inner sleeve of the *Sgt. Pepper* LP glued onto a 'White Album' cover). With this project Chang has turned a commercial pop LP into a 'multiple' work of art. The work was exhibited at Liverpool's FACT gallery in 2014 and is a testimony to the enduring power of the recording, not just its musical adventurousness and diversity but to the superb cover artwork (created by UK artist Richard Hamilton). It is with a consideration of *The Beatles* LP cover then, the first indicator of its break with tradition, that the book begins…

1   http://rutherfordchang.com

'And she's making me feel like I've never been born'

The 'White Album' cover art, from vinyl to digital download

BEN ANDREWS

LENNON: Thinking is weightless
ONO: Use words only for words / things only for things
LOGUE: Wring your hands
PEEL: The revolution is over / we are all free men

John Peel, *Night Ride*, Radios 1 and 2, 12th December 1968, after playing a sequence from Lennon and Ono's *Two Virgins*.[1]

I want to discuss and explore the cover and artwork of the 'White Album' along with the experience of first listening to it on vinyl, a copy from the City of Bath's Music Library, in the early 1980s. This was in the immediate years after John Lennon's assassination, just after I had bought a red 'RIP Bon Scott 1940–1980' t-shirt, along with the Crass' Nagasaki Nightmare a year later, the single released in response to the decision

by the Thatcher government to site American cruise missiles just up the M4 at Greenham Common. The Bath music scene at the time was, apart from the Haydn String Quartet in the Pump Rooms, a mixture of Bristol and Wiltshire Anarcho-punk, Tears for Fears, and pre-Glastonbury warm-up gigs in trendy clubs. Motörhead played the Ace of Spades tour at Bristol Colton Hall and the Stranglers played The Gospel According to the Meninblack tour at the University of Bath. I wasn't allowed to go to either.

So this is a mixture of bedroom recollection, artistic speculation and wildly ambitious analogy, the kind that I hope the late Mark Fisher would have enjoyed. The cover of the 'White Album' looks very strange in the sequence of Beatles' albums, eschewing any immediate signs of marketing or image, and naming itself what one would expect a first album to be named. As the previous album, *Sgt. Pepper's Lonely Hearts Club Band* was the pop art object by Peter Blake, the 'White

---

1   Cavanagh, D. *Good Night and Good Riddance: How thirty-five years of John Peel helped to shape modern life*. London: Faber, 2015, p.61

Album' was a Richard Hamilton-inspired pop-art-meets-the-avant-garde object with a blank or 'industrial' look. Given it was released only a year after both Cream's *Disraeli Gears*, a psychedelic collage of pinks and reds, and The Jimi Hendrix Experiences' *Axis: Bold as Love,* with the band as various incarnations of Vishnu, the 'non-cover' of the 'White Album' is key to understanding the music inside. Its odd song sequencing as odd as another great white double album, Fleetwood Mac's *Tusk*, from 1979.

I'd like to explore the idea that the actual experience of listening to the album is analogous to flicking through the chronologically arranged Beatles' section in the library and coming across the 'White Album', with its blank and distressed cover. Like all good conceptualist anti-art, following Richard Hamilton's hero, Marcel Duchamp, the cover requires the viewer (or listener) to be *interactive*, to work towards completing the meaning of the artwork, photos and collage poster print, by offering a response. When I first saw it, the album certainly looked intriguing, amongst the mock-surrealist and wildly sexist Hipgnosis' artwork for The Scorpions' *Love Drive*, or *Animal Magnetism* or even against the split-screen effect of 10cc's *How Dare You!* of the late seventies, all of which no library user ever appeared to borrow. And

then I want to suggest that interesting things happen to the music when listening to the 'White Album' over the many formats it has been released in since, from double CD, to digital download, to shuffled Spotify playlist.

In November 2016, Scarlett Moffatt, famous from Channel 4's *Gogglebox*, winner of that year's *I'm a Celebrity… Get Me Out of Here!* joined in a conversation with her fellow contestants about time travel and building the Egyptian pyramids.[1] I was watching the show whilst taking a break from writing this and something fell into place about what I wanted to say about the 'White Album'. She added: 'So I think someone from the future realized we'd need them from the future, so went back in time and build the pyramids. And that's why no one knows what technology was used to build them.' (The speed of light being the same first three numbers as the latitude of the top of the largest pyramid.) More later.

It is an interesting contextual digression to note that the Beatles' album of 1968, was recorded under the working title of 'In a Doll's House' or 'Doll's House'[2] before this name

1 http://metro.co.uk/2016/11/16/im-a-celebrity-2016-scarlett-moffatt-gives-her-theory-on-how-time-travel-is-possible-6263267/ accessed Jan 2016
2 Dowling, W.J. *BEATLESONGS*. New York: Simon & Shuster, 1989, p. 220

was shelved. Another British group, Family, had just released an album called *Music in A Doll's House* that same year, a collection of songs on the cusp of an 'almost-concept-album', like The Pretty Thing's *S.F. Sorrow*, released the same week as *The Beatles*, or even The Kink's *The Village Green Preservation Society* of the same year.[1] According to Dowlding 'In a Doll's House' or 'Doll's House' was to be the third album released on the Beatles' Apple label, following George Harrison's *Wonderwall Music* and John and Yoko's *Unfinished Music no.1: Two Virgins*,[2] strengthening Lennon's claim in *Beatles in their Own Words* 'We broke up then'.[3]

Let's look at the political context of the album's release, on the 22nd November 1968. A month earlier, John Peel's Radio 1 *Top Gear* show had to pre-recorded because there were fears that the march to Hyde Park against the Vietnam War, anticipated to be an even more violent re-enactment of the more famous Grosvenor Square rally in the March, would close central London. By the time the show was broadcast, a day ahead of the rally:

Around a thousand students had seized control of the London School of Econom-

ics ahead of... the rally. With students promising an extended sit-in, seminars are held on 'Bourgeois Culture' and 'The Sociology of Revolution'.[4]

Two weeks after the album's November release, John and Yoko appeared on John Peel's *Night Ride* radio programme, where an excerpt from *Two Virgins* is played, after a track from The Deviants, a group from the Ladbrooke Grove squat scene, and the song Wabash Cannonball from a 1956 re-issued The Lonnie Donegan Showcase, finishing with the poet Christopher Logue reading a poem banned from national television, and then Peel-Lennon-Ono-Logue 'conjoin in a... spontaneous... poem of their own', which concludes with Peel's contribution, and above: *'The revolution is over / we are all free men.'*[5]

To understand the significance of *The Beatles*, let's propose that the consumer's initial access to the provocative 'structure of feeling', to use Raymond Williams' term, that the album might be said to articulate is both via its 'blank' artwork and non-sequential naming, and as such stands in every way very much in comparison to its iconic 1967 predecessor, and very much influencing future at-

1 Quantick, D. *Revolution: The Making of the Beatles' White Album*. London: Unanimous, 2002, p.26
2 Dowlding, p.220
3 Dowlding, p.221

4 Cavanagh, p.55
5 Cavanagh p. 58–62

tempts at 'ironic commodity deconstruction' as PiL's *Album* from 1986, *Plastic Box* from 1999; or Durutti Column's debut *The Return of the Durutti Column* from 1980, with sandpaper cover to ruin other records next to it in your collection, or Flipper's debut *Album Generic Flipper* from 1981. Think, even, of the way it might have appeared to a consumer in a record shop in a sequence of the Beatles' discography, as if their covers told the 'story' of the decade, from *Please Please Me*, to *With the Beatles*, to *A Hard Day's Night*, to *Beatles for Sale*, to *Help!*, to *Rubber Soul*, to *Revolver*, to *Sgt. Pepper's Lonely Hearts Club Band*, to *Magical Mystery Tour*, to *Yellow Submarine*, to *The Beatles*.

Sgt. Pepper's Lonely Hearts Club Band seems very contradictory in its visual meanings. However these are interesting contradictions given it is an album that has come to stand in for a certain '1960s moment' in the selective tradition of the music industry and pop iconography that *Mojo* magazine does retrospectives on. What I mean by this is, despite *The Sound of Music* soundtrack LP vastly outselling *Sgt. Pepper*, it has come to represent that decade, it seems self-consciously packaged as a strange 'novelty' commodity-form as if from another era; the four Beatles dressed up in bright Edwardian clothes in the gatefold, the cut-out-and-

keep moustaches of the inner sleeves, and the circus/music hall mode of some of the songs. Whilst at the same time the artwork is very much an attempt at writing a 'new' history from its from cover, one derived by their former selves standing alongside waxworks of countercultural figures from history and the present, it is as if they attempt to write themselves into the counterculture that became less of an 'underground' and more popular culture as the 1960s progressed. By stark contrast, *The Beatles* artwork, appears 'unready', 'unfinished', 'industrial', or even 'conceptual' or interactive'.

If 'In a Doll's House' had been the follow-up to *Sgt. Pepper*, it might have sounded and looked much more like a dark version of an 'almost-concept-album' of its iconic pop art predecessor. However, there are song remnants of the lost conceptual continuity of 'In a Doll's House' on *The Beatles*: the creepy descriptions of big houses and séances in Cry Baby Cry, with its nursery rhyme 'sing a song of sixpence' reference and scolding chorus and 'mysterious laughter behind half open doors',[1] just before the spoken word ending of 'Come along children, its off to bed' of earlier versions of Good Night, or juxtaposed with Honey Pie, one of Paul's 'gran-

---

1 MacDonald, I. *Revolution in the Head: The Beatles' Records and the Sixties*. London: Pimlico, 1995, p.239.

ny songs' according to Lennon, could have set the scene well for an album of slightly sinister up-tight Victoriana, with an 'I miss my mother' song in Julia. The sequence of the different styles of songs from the trite singalong of Ob-La-Di, Ob-La-Da, the loud knees-up of Birthday, the disorientation beyond-control on the spiral slide of an English funfair, Helter Skelter[1], and the lullaby Good Night[2] could skilfully recreate the disorienting passage of a child through the rooms of a sprawling doll's house. The harsh juxtaposition of songs styles might have also recreated a creepy ellipses between rooms, as if no one communicates or each room tries to ignore or turn its back on the other. Even the Romantic simplicity of a song about a bird in Blackbird, with added bird noises, seems apt for an album set in some version of childhood, imagining yourself outside its confines; and even the purposely childlike and sinister Piggies, with added pig noises and manic harpsichord, might fit. Honey Pie even, with its foxtrot stage band instrumentation and scratchy 78 rpm gramophone-effects, has a haunted drawing room feel to it.

I think this would have been a superb Beatles album. However, during the recording, at some time roughly when George Martin took

off on holiday ('I tried to plead with them to be selective and make it a really good single album, but they wouldn't have it') and at some time roughly when Ringo walked out of the studio refusing to play his drums, and at some time roughly when Yoko Ono moved her bed into the recording studio, it became something better than that. What might the cover have looked like? Maybe something like the painted walls of 'Kinfauns', George Harrison's bungalow at 16 Claremont Drive, Esher, Surrey: flowers and suns and mandalas. Most early demos for the album were rehearsed here.

So the cover of the original record unlike most albums, is able to emphasize the passage of time since it was first bought, the circular shape of the vinyl wearing through the cover, parts of the The Beatles' lettering frayed off, the spine on the inner gatefold slightly mildewed, the top loading slits for the vinyl frayed. As such, the cover resembles Robert Rauschenberg's 'White Paintings' from 1951, which John Cage describes in Silence as 'airports for the lights, shadows and particles'. Just as 'White Paintings' pick up the weather and gallery dust, so the 'White Album' in vinyl format picks up visible time. Remembering Laura Moffatt's speculation about the pyramids, time is an important theme. It is as if the 'White Album'

1 MacDonald, p. 240 fn.1
2 Dowlding p. 220

anticipated the end of its format, to a time after Side 1, Side 2 etc. to the random shuffle play of a streaming playlist, the latest format that I 'have' the 'White Album' in. Even on CD, the side ordering starts to disappear. Musically, the non-sequential nature of the ordering of the songs, the lack of attempting to make the double album appear to 'flow' or progress and the almost deliberate juxtaposition of styles leads to this expansive feeling, braking out of its commodity-form, only realized in digital era's lack or lessening of the original vinyl sides. It is almost as if the experience of listening to the 'White Album' anticipated opening listeners to the juxtapositions of a random digital sequence, i.e. Spotify's shuffle play. Given this, there is a point to recording Good Night 'overlush'. Lennon asked George Martin to 'Arrange it like Hollywood. Yeah, corny'; after Revolution 9, an ironic ending to settle the listeners down, like Ringo mock-patronising the 'revolutionary' children, as if to say 'you've had your fun'.

Thinking about the political context of the album again, if *Sgt Pepper* was an album Devin McKinney describes in *Magic Circles: The Beatles in Dream and History*, as:

> the most brilliant fake in rock and roll history — Beatles behind the curtains, pulling the strings... But a fake of its time... the bright shiny lie they offered to the world — and themselves! — that such a utopia of mind, body, and spirit as the album represented was the natural and only possible culmination of all that proceeded it. But the record's falseness was not solely their doing... the hippies, already mounting their own cover up, ratified the Beatles: in their collective hands, 1967 emerged as a paradisal fantasy of unity.

The 'White Album', mimicking the jarring eclecticism of a good John Peel radio show, is also the break up album: 'We broke up then'. One last comment on the album's cover should note that in India, where most of the songs were written, white is the colour of mourning. So whereas a Westerner might see the cover as being an ironic anti-commercial joke, there is a hidden Indian connection, that of death and an opening to reincarnated rebirth.

Back in the U.S.S.R.

DAVID KEREKES

The year is 2008. The location is the College Arms, a central London pub with a refreshing lack of through-traffic for a Saturday afternoon. The staff busies itself with odd jobs and gaze out the window.

Two young men enter the pub and head to the only occupied table. They have a cordial greeting for those at the table, me and a bunch of mates, and from a leather shoulder bag one takes a book and passes it round. The book is a slim paperback called *Chant and be Happy: The Power of Meditation*.[1]

It's been years since I last witnessed the Hare Krishnas buttonholing in this fashion, albeit never before in a pub. When I was a teenager in Manchester, they were often dancing and chanting on Deansgate or through St Anne's Square in sandals and robes. Not as common a sight in London in 2008. But while times have changed, *Chant and be Happy*, which I now flick through, appears in stasis.

A recent edition of the book, from last year, I see in its pages exactly what I saw when I first saw it. *Chant and be Happy* encompasses the teachings of His Divine Grace A.C. Bhaktivedanta Swami Prabhupada, who adorns the cover. The topic is the search for happiness and how best to chant. On the back cover are pictures of two Beatles: John Lennon and George Harrison.

Why the Beatles? Early in 1968, extolling the virtues of Transcendental Meditation and the Hare Krishna mantra as the path to peace and liberation (as they did LSD), the Beatles travelled to a retreat in Rishikesh in India. Their guru was the Maharishi Mahesh Yogi, with whom they sought greater heights of spiritual awareness. But ultimately they were letdown, determining that the Maharishi's goal was altogether earthbound as he had quite a fondness for the ladies.

In Rishikesh and at home soon afterwards the Beatles created a lot of new music, much of it to appear later that year on *The Beatles*, the album more commonly known

1 *Chant and be Happy: The Power of Meditation. the teachings of His Divine Grace A.C. Bhaktivedanta Swami Prabhupada*. The Bhaktivedanta Book Trust, 2014. Copyright 1982, 2009.

as the 'White Album'.

In the College Arms I am excited that *Chant and be Happy* features the Beatles, that a band that split almost a half-century ago is still considered key.

Harrison and Lennon were the most vocal exponents of Krishna Consciousness. Ringo Starr didn't much care for it and found the retreat in Rishikesh much like Butlin's; McCartney, well I don't know what McCartney made of it, likely he was unimpressed. It is no surprise therefore that Lennon and Harrison adorn the back cover, their portraits the same long-hair portraits as appear in the 'White Album'. Inside the book are more Beatle images, along with quotations and a long interview with Harrison about Hare Krishna and his solo hit of 1971, the mystical My Sweet Lord.

I am enlightened and entertained. This is not 1968, but 2008, and yet the emphasis of *Chant and be Happy* is on the Beatles, as if the Beatles are the next big thing, as if the band is a clarion call for disillusioned people everywhere. There is no evidence here that Lennon and Harrison are both dead.

I give the Hare Krishna fellows the suggested donation of £3 without quibble. It's not often these days one gets to donate to a cause championed by the Fab Four.

The Beatles are a transcendent force, remaining so. Their knack is to somehow encapsulate the purpose of existence in a solitary chord, a gift like great surgeons have or those people who move objects with their minds, which is perhaps a lofty statement for four lads from the north of England and yet at the same time entirely true.

The opening track on the 'White Album' is Back In The U.S.S.R., a track not significant in the way that perhaps Tomorrow Never Knows is significant, in that it doesn't forge a new direction in popular music and by virtue alter Western consciousness in the twentieth century (per Ian McDonald in *Revolution in the Head*). Rather it features the sound of a jet plane touching down on a runway at the start of the song and then intermittently throughout its 2'43" running time. The song is a simple sort of pop-rock song, with nice harmonies. But imagine a Geiger counter: Beatles songs, even the outwardly simple ones such as this, are much like evidence of plutonium, in that the needle goes crazy when you get close.

Back In The U.S.S.R. and its screeching refrain is the sound of the everyday, what ear specialists warn you about when they warn you about noise, and it is the sound of a Starbucks, the scraw of coffee percolating, which is much like the sound of the jet plane landing and what I hear as I write this, and the people around me who make flight plans for their summer holidays. Someone wearing a Beatles t-shirt chides his children for taking too much chocolate topping.

That needle, jumping forward and back.

The actor Warren Mitchell said in one of those pop culture talking-head type television shows, this one about racism in the 1970s, that some people misinterpreted Alf Garnett, the fictional character he played in the comedy show *Till Death Do Us Part*. Some people, he said, did not consider Alf Garnett a bigot, or ironic in any way, but rather that the character spoke the truth when he talked down about race. The response of Warren Mitchell to those people was simple. 'You're an idiot,' he told them. 'Alf Garnett is about people like you.'

I want to leave Back In The U.S.S.R. a moment for another Beatles track. The song is Get Back, an early working version of which exists on bootleg and, at the time of writing, also on YouTube, where it is afforded the title Commonwealth. The origins of Common-

wealth/Get Back are a spontaneous jam in one of the Beatles' final sessions together.

As with much material that emerged from the so-called Twickenham sessions, a low point for the band as a creative unit, Commonwealth derives from observations made by the band about last night's telly. The inspiration in this instance was right wing politics, with references to then Prime Minister Harold Wilson and MPs Edward Heath and Enoch Powell, soon to be famous for his Rivers of Blood speech.

More ambiguous is a later version of the same song, the structure and melody by now recognizable as the Get Back we all know. McCartney, whose song it is, paraphrases again the political discourse of the day. 'Immigrants' are told to 'get back.' Alas, any reference to Enoch Powell is absent now, leaving McCartney alone at the helm; these words his words. This proto Get Back was never intended for release. It is a work in progress.

Viewed in context, we can apply Warren Mitchell's Alf Garnett appellation, *you're an idiot; the song is all about people like you*.

But knowing this information, knowing the genus of a song that is loved the world over — considered by and large innocent — proves the undercurrent that helps make the Beatles such a dichotomy.

Despite the singsong melodies and the commercial discography this to me is not a commercial band in the usual sense. Eyebrows invariably rise at a song rooted in right wing politics, but they don't at what Get Back would become, odd enough itself because what it becomes is a song about a transsexual drug runner.

The needle bouncing forward and back.

That's Get Back. Pinging in all directions is Back In The U.S.S.R. with a politic of its own. The song is structured as a pastiche of the Beach Boys, an all-American band for whom summer was endless and filled with surfboards and convertible-top motorcars. The pastiche is patently clear, because, as the title of the song suggests, Back In The U.S.S.R. is not about America or the values of the free world but about the Soviet Union. The singer, McCartney again, sings in the first person of a bumpy BOAC flight, during which he sits with a paper bag on his knee. But arriving in the harsh Soviet climate, on hearing balalaikas ringing out, he considers himself home and a very lucky man indeed.

So on the one hand, Back In The U.S.S.R. is a pastiche of the Beach Boys (a member of the Beach Boys having apparently put the idea to the Beatles in the first place), but we might also consider it a song about racial harmony: those in the East having the same needs as the people in the west.

As I write this a Lennon and McCartney songwriting trait comes to mind. Rarely was the duo's work a 50/50 split, despite the joint songwriting credit. Lennon in a song never seems to know what he wants. When advocating revolution, for instance, he demands to be counted in… and out (Revolution No.1); when he thinks no one is in his tree, he also thinks his tree must be high or low (Strawberry Fields Forever); when he reaches out to his dead mother, what he says is that half of what he says is meaningless (Julia).

McCartney by contrast writes songs that are a finger jab in the proverbial sides, first positing an idea and then confounding the listener with it. Love songs, for McCartney, are double-edged swords. He's going to grow old and retire with the one he loves, but will his love still need him or still feed him when he's sixty-four (When I'm Sixty-Four)? Back In The U.S.S.R. is like this. Outwardly playful, we think we have a measure of the song when suddenly that finger comes poking.

Sneers McCartney in the run up to the chorus: 'You don't know how lucky you are, *boy*.'

In 1965, the Rev David A Noebell identified a virulent strain of anti-American ideals in popular music. In a pamphlet, *Communism, Hypnotism and The Beatles*,[1] he considered the Fab Four in context of a particular form of children's record that he called 'sleepy time' music. Mothers everywhere had for years used sleepy time records to help put their children to sleep at night. The Beatles, stated the Rev Noebell, were now doing much the same for Western teenagers, brainwashing them with their insidious melodies and inducing them to sleepwalk into communism.

Back In The U.S.S.R. was not recorded when the best-selling pamphlet first saw print, but it's safe to assume that the Rev Noebell suffered conniptions when finally he heard it, proof positive of what he had been preaching all along.

Noebell's argument is not unique. Yellow Submarine is an earlier example of a song

indicative of supposed communist ties, in this instance the Beatles and Red China. 'Our friends are all aboard…. everyone one of us has all we need… we all live in a yellow submarine.' Before that, in 1966, Lennon's proclamation that the Beatles were more popular than Jesus resulted in a backlash within America's Christian Right, culminating with the public burning of Beatles records.

According to Noebell, the Beatles are leading us to 'cybernetic warfare'. While this makes for an entertaining read, with credible diversions into the theories of Pavlov and Aristotle, ultimately it's not possible to join the dots the way Noebell sees them. His expression for America's youth, quantifying them as 'our teenager,' carries its own unsettling connotations and is perhaps the most telling aspect of his twenty-eight-page pamphlet.

If Noebell had been granted an insight into how the East perceived the Beatles during this era of Cold War politics, he would have seen a mirror inversion of his own ideas. The Beatles never performed behind the Iron Curtain and, apart from one track on a music and folk compilation in 1967, credited to the 'Beatles quartet', their music was not officially available there until some years after they disbanded. The Beatles were considered by the Kremlin a key exponent of West-

---

1 Noebel, Rev. David A., *Communism, Hypnotism and the Beatles: An Analysis of the Communist Use of Music — The Communist Master Music Plan*. Oaklahoma: Christian Crusade Publications, 1965. If the figures cited in the edition I have seen are accurate, the pamphlet made it to a fourth printing at least, by which point 55,000 copies were in circulation. Noebel himself was still penning right-wing Christian tracts through to 2010, a couple more of them expanding on the Beatles menace.

ern decadence, and unhealthy for young Soviet minds.

My father wasn't born in the Soviet Union, but in a country near enough under the same iron fist. He had never heard any Western music until he was sixteen, the age he was when he escaped to the west. All he knew about the west up to that point was Cowboys and Indians. Cowboys and Indians were considered indicative of democratic failings, and therefore a permissible topic for the Eastern Bloc. He also knew the expression 'coals to Newcastle' for much the same reason: the hardworking proletariat crushed beneath the wheels of capitalism. Otherwise nothing of the west was discussed or taught in Hungarian schools in the 1940s and 1950s. History books contained nothing of the achievements of the free world. Instead my father and his classmates had to do things like observe Joseph Stalin's death with a three-minute silence.

At the first opportunity he joined the revolution, the revolution that took him out of communism, and to the revolution that was Elvis waiting for teenagers on the other side.

He thought Back In The U.S.S.R. a weird thing to joke about. It stopped my father in his tracks when he first heard me playing it — much as the Sex Pistols would stop him years later — and he said without irony, 'What do they know about communism?'

That's the Geiger counter, the needle bouncing forward and back.

McCartney became the first and only Beatle to play Russia, on a concert tour in 2003 that concluded in Red Square. The show was met by an incredulous audience, sort of Beatlemania lite but with grown men reduced to tears. A highlight of the show was Back In The U.S.S.R., part of an encore that began with the jet plane squeal so familiar now.

A concert film of the Russia tour, released shortly afterwards, won plaudits. In it are conversations with Beatles fans who grew up behind the Iron Curtain, who admit to listening to Beatles songs in secret via black market records and forbidden radio broadcasts from the west. To do otherwise under communist rule would have landed them in trouble.

I can imagine then, with this history, in these circumstances and against this backdrop, Back In The U.S.S.R. in Red Square in 2003 must have been akin to a peak experience.

The Soviet Union no longer exists but here is

that song, the redaction of its ashes, and in a way the ultimate pop culture hat trick.

McCartney in Russia is a guest of President Vladimir Putin, who is seen in attendance at the Red Square concert. The Rev Noebell would not have approved, and likely neither would former KGB officer Putin back in the day. But, to quote the sociologist at the beginning of the concert film, the Beatles 'have done more for the fall of Communism than any other western institution.' That's no mean feat for sleepy time music. No mean feat for a pop-rock song of the Beatles that has no high aspirations, not like Tomorrow Never Knows.

The song is also missing the compelling lineage of Get Back, although one might direct it toward the Rev Noebell and to Putin and say to them: *you're an idiot; this song is for you*.

Back In The U.S.S.R. is a transcendent force. It opens *The Beatles*, the album more commonly known as the 'White Album', which is an album full of interesting doors.

Dear Prudence

MELISSA MAPLES

The '23 enigma' centres around the idea that everything in the world is somehow connected by the number 23. Believers can cite countless instances that they feel are evidence of this connection. There are 23 pairs of chromosomes in human DNA. The sum of the first 23 prime numbers is 874, which is divisible by 23. Julius Caesar was stabbed 23 times. The 23rd letter of the English alphabet, W, has 2 points down and 3 points up.

Charles Manson was born on the 12th of November, i.e. the 11th month. 12 + 11 = 23.

There is a natural tendency for the human brain to fabricate connections between unrelated pieces of information. This attempt to create meaning out of randomness is a type of coping mechanism, designed to help us feel like we have a manageable and defined role in the universe. In general these thought patterns are harmless, and for many people they can even be helpful in terms of quelling anxiety. For others, though, the creation of these false connections gets out of control, and crosses over into a type of psychotic delusion referred to as *apophaenia*.

Charles Manson himself based much of his belief system on synchronistic ideas powered by overzealous selective perception. Specifically, he felt there were clues in the 'White Album' that tied in with the Book of Revelation and the concept of Armageddon, as if the Beatles were sending coded instructions down the record grooves for how the End of Days was to manifest. Furthermore, Manson thought his unique ability to bring all these puzzle pieces together into a cohesive narrative demonstrated that he, meaning he specifically, was destined to be the catalyst of an upcoming apocalyptic racial war, which he thought was predicted in the parallels he found between Beatles lyrics and Biblical scripture.

In February of 1968, when Manson was still building the foundations of his dark empire, Prudence Farrow found herself engulfed in a more peaceful darkness — the deep, quiet clarity of meditation. The younger sister of actress Mia Farrow had joined a group of high-profile travellers, including the Beatles, on a journey to India to learn advanced Transcendental Meditation from Maharishi Mahesh Yogi. Prudence had latched onto the technique more readily than the others, and although the sun was up and the sky was blue, she preferred to shut herself away in her cottage, meditating alone for days on end and rarely coming out. Three weeks into her self-imposed exile, John Lennon was asked to reach out to her and encourage her to rejoin the group and socialise a bit more. Lennon wrote the song Dear Prudence in response, a reminder to Farrow that she was 'part of everything', along with a request to 'open up your eyes' and 'see the sunny skies'.

In the context of Charles Manson's madness and apophaenic tendencies, the cheerful, optimistic disposition of Dear Prudence drew less of his attention than other tracks on the 'White Album'. That said, the song became legendary in its own right after the Tate-LaBianca murders in 1969, when the entire world became aware of Manson's deeds and his obsession with the 'White Album'. Curious onlookers started matching up the songs on the album to their own observations, and the spooky coincidences surrounding Dear Prudence and Manson soon rivalled the 23 enigma in terms of volume and reach. In writing out the facts and marking the overlaps, it's easy to see how something as manufactured as confirmation bias can start to look more like Satan's experimental art project.

To note a few examples:

❑ In 1968, Roman Polanski directed *Rosemary's Baby*. He initially thought someone like Sharon Tate would fit well in the title role, but studio executives wanted a more famous actress to play Rosemary, eventually settling on Mia Farrow, a household name (and the sister of Prudence Farrow).

❑ Polanski married Sharon Tate in 1968. The following year, Tate became the most famous victim of the Manson Family's murder spree.

❑ *Rosemary's Baby* is a story about a pregnant woman victimised by evil people. Sharon Tate was pregnant with Polanski's child at the time she was murdered by Manson's followers.

❑ During filming, Polanski instructed Mia Farrow to walk into real New York City traffic. When Farrow hesitated, Polanski waved off her concerns and told her that 'no one's going to hit a pregnant woman'.

❑ The Dakota building in New York City was used for filming the exteriors of the fictional Bramford building in *Rosemary's Baby*. Twelve years after the film was made, John Lennon was murdered in front of the Dakota, where he was living at the time.

❑ In 1973, John Lennon attended a party in California, during which he allegedly flew into an uncontrolled rage. Afterward, several partygoers reported that Lennon had smashed mirrors, thrown a chair out of a window, broken a television by hurling it against a wall, and screamed that 'this is all Roman Polanski's fault'. Lennon never commented on this episode, and it is not known what he meant by the alleged Polanski comment.

One of the more chilling links between Prudence Farrow and the Manson ethos came to light in a *Rolling Stone* interview in 2015. Interviewer David Chiu asked Farrow about the first time she'd ever heard the song Dear Prudence, when her mother played it for her in New York City. According to Farrow, her mother had put on a copy of the then-recently-released 'White Album' at a family gathering, and used the music as a soundtrack for a bizarre game the family played called 'killer', in which one player commits symbolic mass murder on all the others.

'It's kind of like a psychological game. The

person winks at you, and then you wait, and you have to sort of gauge who it is. But you never want to catch everybody's eyes because they could wink at you and you're dead. It was the perfect opportunity for [my mother] to go and "kill" everybody. So she went around to everybody saying this song is coming up next. She put it on, and she went around preparing everybody, but she was "killing" them. She came to me while the song [Dear Prudence] was playing. She said, "Isn't it beautiful?" I looked up, and she gave me a wink.'

All games aside, it's worth mentioning that Farrow has also had very real personal brushes with darkness and murder. In 1979, she began an extramarital affair with New York City heir Robert Durst, who was also married at the time. In January of 1982, Farrow ended the relationship. Three days later, Durst's wife Kathie disappeared, and has never been found. Over the years, Durst has been a person of interest in numerous suspicious deaths and disappearances, and was the subject of the HBO documentary series *The Jinx*, after which he was arrested and charged with murdering his long-time friend, Susan Berman. In 2003, Prudence Farrow even asked law enforcement authorities for help, as she was afraid of Durst and feared for her safety.

One might think that nearly fifty years on from the 'White Album' and the Manson murders, the power of the imagined connections between the two would have faded, the spell irrevocably broken by the clarity of hindsight. However, online forums and websites devoted to exploring these topics demonstrate that people are still fascinated by the idea of interweaving them. Perhaps it's simply the way the human brain processes the tragedies of the past, combined with a societal tendency toward a oddly morbid romantic memory. Or perhaps, like Prudence Farrow, our perpetual inclination is to withdraw and look deeper, even when we are invited to come outside and enjoy the sunshine.

Glass Onion

PATRICK SEVC

The Beatles. The 'laughing freemen' of the 1960s. The megalithic rock group beloved by all. Their personalities and music are undeniably imbued with a certain magic that set them apart from the rest. And yet something mysterious and uncanny seems to always linger, almost imperceptibly, in the periphery of their works. For example, most Beatles enthusiasts have at least heard about such things as the rumour that Paul McCartney died, playing their songs backwards to hear messages pertaining to this, as well as the visual clues on their album covers, and Charles Manson's obsession with them, to name a few.

Are there really any significant symbolisms in their lyrics and album covers? Is this larger-than-life pop group all it really seems on the surface? Let's peel away at these enigmatic onion skins and look below the exterior of these iconic men and their iconic works.

In order to do so, however, it is important to begin with a proper foundation of mythology. But who has time for mythology, right?

From a 2000 article on Stanley Kubrick from *Vanity Fair* Magazine:

> *When Kubrick sent you a book, he wanted you to read it, and not just read it, but to drop everything and get into it. John Calley, who was probably Stanley's closest friend, told me that when he was head of production at Warners in the seventies and first working with him, Stanley sent him a set of Frazer's* The Golden Bough, *unabridged, and then bugged him every couple of weeks for a year about reading it. Finally Calley said, 'Stanley, I've got a studio to run. I don't have time to read mythology.' 'It isn't mythology, John,' Stanley said. 'It's your life.'*

The concepts described in *The Golden Bough* are exactly those which one needs to understand in order to allow the themes the Beatles were working with. Namely the longstanding, world-wide traditions of the Dying God, the King Kill and the scapegoat. Many cultures for thousands of years have held the tradition of a wandering outsider, or slave, killing the king and marrying his daughter in order to keep the bloodline, and thus the kingdom, fresh.

It is likewise just as important for one to understand the concept of the Thelemic Aeons: The first Aeon of mankind was that of Isis, the Mother. The era of the fertility goddess. The second was that of Osiris, the Dying God. The Paternal age. The Christian era. Occultist and founder of Thelema, Aleister Crowley, who also appears in the top left corner of the *Sgt. Pepper* cover crowd, states in his book *The Book of the Law*, that we are now entering the Aeon of Horus, that of the Crowned and Conquering Child. The previous era, the Christian era, the Aeon of Osiris, unfolded through enigmatic parables. And so it seems the Aeon of Horus may be unfolding through media culture, namely enigmatic films and pop groups.

Any Beatles fan would say one of, if not the most highly enigmatic lines in the Beatles canon is Lennon's 'I am the walrus'. What does he mean by that? Why does he, a year later, in the song Glass Onion, tell us now that 'the walrus was Paul'? Why have they traded places?

The key to this conundrum cryptically hides at the centre of all Beatles enigmas. The Sgt. Pepper drum. It, of course, reads in stylized letters 'Sgt. Pepper's Lonely Hearts Club Band', the name of their 1967 album. However, hold a mirror horizontally to the middle of the drum, so that 'LONELY HEARTS' becomes reflected onto itself, and 'LONELY HEARTS' becomes '1ONE1X HE^DIE', with the arrow pointing up to Paul. An indisputable cipher lodged into the centre of their artwork. The other important thing to note, which is often overlooked, is that the L and H of 'LONELY HEARTS' alphanumerically equals 12/8, the date Lennon died. So with this oracular drum skin, we have the deaths of both McCartney and Lennon being alluded to.

But what about the walrus?

The Latin name for walrus is *Odobenus Rosmarus Divergens*. 'Rosmarus' comes from the Norse word for 'Horse of the Sea'. Among the crowd of cut-outs on the cover of *Sgt. Pepper's*, we have Tim Carey from Stanley Kubrick's 1956 film *The Killing* (though Carey ended up being hidden behind George Harrison). The word 'occult' means 'hidden', so let's assume there could be some importance, or hidden wisdom, to be gleaned from the cut-outs that ended up being obscured on the *Sgt. Pepper* cover. After all, symbolism is much more effective subliminally — or hidden in plain sight. The scene in which Tim Carey's cut-out is from is the one where he is shooting a race horse. Carey is hidden behind George, with his gun behind Paul's head, which is aimed at John. The two main characters in *The Killing* are George and Johnny. George shoots all of the characters except Johnny.

On December 8th, 1980, John Lennon was gunned down outside his home at the Dakota building in New York City by a deranged fan named Mark David Chapman. This young man also happened to be obsessed with J.D. Salinger's book *The Catcher in the Rye*, which is adorned with an illustration of a carousel horse on the cover. Combining the topics of Rosmarus the 'Horse of the Sea', and the Dakota, one's thoughts turn toward Roman Polanski's film which was shot at the Dakota, *Rosemary's Baby*. The name Rosemary means 'Dew of the Sea'. Interestingly, Mia Farrow, who accompanied the Beatles in India, stars as the voice of *The Last Unicorn*, in which she, as the last unicorn, another kind of horse, must save the rest of her kind, all trapped in the ocean as the dew of the sea.

Pretty soon you're gonna be dead.

The above line is from Lennon's hit song In-

stant Karma. The very song which Stephen King named his novel *The Shining* after, with its line 'We all shine on, like the moon and the stars and the sun.' King's story is about a boy who sees visions of bloodshed. Stanley Kubrick's film version was released in May of 1980 in America, November 7th in the UK. In the beginning, little Danny's mother Wendy reads *Catcher in the Rye*. It is immediately after she reads from this book that Danny sees the large pool of blood pour from the elevator of the hotel he is about to live in during the winter of 1980.

Danny's backwards-written message 'REDRUM' needs to be mirrored in order to be deciphered. (Redrum could also be seen as 'read drum'). Red Rum was the name of one of the most famous thoroughbreds of our time, who dominated the horse racing world in the 1970s. Incidentally, the name Wendy was first used in literature in *Peter Pan*. J.D. Salinger's exposition of *Catcher in the Rye* is titled The Last and Best of the Peter Pans, and according to his instructions is not due to be published for some time.

Of all the topics brought up so far; the walrus, the mirror and the mixed identities bring to mind none other than Tweedledee & Tweedledum, the two curious figures who cross paths with Alice while on the other side of the looking glass and tell her the story of The Walrus and the Carpenter. They are two distinct individuals, but essentially one entity in many ways. We all know that the Beatles wore their Lewis Carroll influence on their psychedelic sleeves in 1967 as well as on the 'White Album' in 1968.

Another famous incident of mixed identities are those of Rosencratnz and Guildenstern in Shakespeare's *Hamlet*. Two friends of Prince Hamlet's who are sent to their deaths by Hamlet as his scapegoats. In 1966, Tom Stoppard's comedic play *Rosencrantz and Guildenstern Are Dead* was debuted in Edinburgh, which follows the exploits of these two characters as they weave in and out of the original play. The fact that nobody is sure which is Rosencrantz and which is Guildenstern is amped up in this spoof.

In 1964, the Beatles performed a televised skit from Shakespeare's *A Midsummer Night's Dream*. They spoof the play within the play 'Pyramus and Thisbe' (Act V, Scene 1). McCartney as Pyramus kills himself at the end, and upon such discovery, Lennon as Thisbe in turn also commits suicide. It is Rosencrantz and Guildenstern who provide Hamlet with travelling play actors with which Hamlet uses to re-enact the death of his father, the King, in hopes of discovering the

guilt of his uncle, Claudius, whom he suspects is the murderer.

Odobenus from the Latin name for walrus means 'walks on teeth'. Most Beatles fans are aware that McCartney chipped his left front tooth in December 1965. It was fixed later in 1966, but the chip is visible in the promo films for Rain and Paperback Writer. Oddly enough, in the Pyramus & Thisbe skit, Lennon has his left front tooth blackened out. Roman Polanski loses said tooth in his film *The Tenant*.

Curiously, 1990 saw the release of a film version of Rosencrantz and Guildenstern Are Dead. In 2009, a film titled *Rosencrantz and Guildenstern are Undead* was released. The soundtrack was written and recorded by Sean Lennon.

Ringo starrs in *The Magic Christian* with Peter Sellers. The first thing the two do after Sellers adopts Ringo is go to see a performance of *Hamlet*. They arrive late and are told that they are at the part with Rosencrantz and Guildenstern. Shortly thereafter, Hamlet (played by Laurence Harvey, the Manchurian candidate in *The Manchurian Candidate*), does a strip tease and a large star-shaped sign is lowered towards the stage which reads 'Zap' in lights. And incidentally, in the

Beatles' 1964 film *A Hard Day's Night*, while looking into a mirror and surrounded by men in military marching band uniforms, McCartney recites the line from Hamlet, 'Oh, that this too, too solid flesh would melt.' He then turns quickly to the camera and exclaims 'Zap!'

Now we must turn to the other pillar of resource for European mysticism, Egyptian mythology. Namely we turn to Aker, the double lion god, guardian of the portals to the Underworld. The Egyptians believed that Aker guarded the gates of dawn and sunset through which the sun rose every morning and set every evening. Statues of Aker often were given the heads of men and women, which the ancient Greeks referred to as sphinxes, in reference to the Greek legend of the Sphinx who artistically concealed truth within riddles and puns.

The Aker statues were 'keepers who open and shut the gates, into the worlds of Yesterday, Today and Tomorrow.' The two twin lions were named Sef (Yesterday) and Duau (Today). Beatles fans are familiar with the 1966 American release of the Beatles album *Yesterday And Today*, which was originally adorned with the infamous 'Butcher' cover in which the Beatles are wearing lab coats and are draped with fourteen pieces of meat,

harkening to legends of the dismembered Osiris. Tides of disgust spurred Capitol Records to call back the LPs and reissue them with a new cover image. So, they were out of the woods, right? Well, the replacement cover featured McCartney sitting within a large chest, harkening to legends of Osiris being locked into a chest. Lennon sits upon the chest with legs crossed in the tarot Hanged Man fashion.

The way things are going, they're gonna crucify me.

So, who is the walrus? Lennon or McCartney? The Hebrew word for walrus is Yem Sus, which also means 'Horse of the Sea'. Sus meaning Horse. The English word Jesus comes from a corrupted Greek version of the name Yeheshua; Iosus, which actually translates to 'Man Horse'.

Seems whichever is the walrus, the other is the carpenter — which can easily be taken metaphorically as the Christ. With Christ, we have the quintessential dying god archetypal figure. The scapegoat of the world.

According to astrological symbolism, the Christian eon corresponds to the age of Pisces, because the spring-point has been passing through the constellation of Pisces during the Christian eon, and the first fish in that constellation has been associated with Christ, and the second fish has been associated with Anti-Christ.

Carl Jung states it's a matter of astrological fact that the spring-point entered the second fish around the 16th century, around the time of the Reformation and the Renaissance. With these comes the spirit which culminates in the modern age, the spirit of Anti-Christ. An intellectual, Promethian, Luciferian enlightenment rather than a spiritual enlightenment.

It should be noted here that the Hebrew letter Nun also translates to Fish, and that Nun is the letter attributed to the Death card of the tarot, which incidentally commonly features a horse. Jungian scholar Edward Edinger states that the Christian myth has an enantiodromia built into it; the turning into an opposite. The New Testament predicts that Christ will be followed by the Anti-Christ.

'Give us Barabbas!'

There is also the matter of Jesus and Barabbas essentially having the same name. Barabbas' full name was Jesus Barrabbas. Later, the Jesus part was dropped, as Jesus became a sacred word. Literally

Barabbas means 'son of the Father'. It was a common name, but here it takes on a significant irony. The crowd must choose between the two Jesuses, both of whom are a 'son of the Father'. Jesus was an innocent man about to be murdered, and Barabbas was a murderer about to be set free. The Jews reject Jesus, the son of God, and instead they take Jesus, the son of the Father (John 8:44). If we consider the story of Barabbas from the Gnostic point of view, both Jesus and Barabbas represent two elements of the same person. Jesus represents nature's higher plane, the creative consciousness. Barabbas represents the violent force of nature, the lower plane, which man chose.

Aleister Crowley called himself The Beast. His disciple Jack Parsons called himself The Anti-Christ. Who then is the False Prophet? The Messiah or the Aeon of Horus?

Watch out for false prophets. They come to you in sheep's clothing, but inwardly they are ferocious wolves. By their fruit you will recognize them. Matthew 7:15

The Christ and the Devil, the ultimate archetypal depictions of good vs. evil. Interestingly, the Hebrew word Nachash, which means The Serpent (of the Garden), has the Gematrical value of 358. The Hebrew word for Messiah, Meshiach, also equals 358. 3, 5 and 8 are the 5th, 6th and 7th letters of the Fibonacci sequence. Interesting, since lightning and trees branch out in accordance with the Fibonacci sequence. Kabbalah depicts creation as lightning descending down the Tree of Life — and in turn, according to European mysticism, the serpent ascends to the top. When Hebrew words share the same Gematrical value, it is not a coincidence; it means they are meant to be viewed in the same light.

The 16th century German thaler coin, where we get our word and symbol for the dollar, depicts a serpent on a cross on one side and Jesus on a cross on the other. The English word Fool comes from the Latin root follis, which means leather bag or bellows for stoking fires. And is also used with a sense of 'windbag or air-headed person'. Additionally, follis was used to describe a leather bag containing a specific amount of coins. Crowley emphasized this connection in his tarot deck by depicting the Fool carrying a bag of coins. Furthermore, the Fool card of the tarot is attributed to the Hebrew letter Aleph, which means Life Breath, tying back into the air and wind themes of the Vulgar Latin usage of follis.

I told you about the fool on the hill.

Somewhat recently, the lyrics to Fool On The Hill written in Lennon's handwriting have surfaced, inciting speculation into his authorship of the song. Regardless, we have Lennon and McCartney as the archetypal fools. Added to the fact that Lennon wears a motley jacket while singing his nonsensical lyrics during I Am The Walrus.

'My Prophet is a Fool with his 111.' says Aiwass, the entity who allegedly dictated The Book Of The Law to Crowley. The numerical value of the Hebrew word Aleph is 111. 'One and one and one is three.' 'Got to be a joker he just do what he please.'

In Hebrew legend, one brings a Golem to life by writing the word for 'Truth' on its forehead. The word in Hebrew is AMT, Aleph Mem, Tav (pronounced Emet). Aleph, Mem and Tav are the first, middle and last letters of the Hebrew alphabet. When one is done with the Golem, its life is ended by erasing the Aleph. AMT without the Aleph is MET, which is the Hebrew word for 'Death'. In other words, you have literally removed the life force from the Golem, and now have death. (The Beatles' most famous American concert was held at Shea Stadium, home of the NY Mets, who had a miraculous season in 1969, winning the World Series, which began on October 11th, the day before the PID rumour went viral, October 12th, which is Aleister Crowley's birthday).

The Hebrew word ADM, or ADAM, means 'Aleph In Blood'. *111 in blood*.

The Golem is created in the pattern of the Adam. In *Rosemary's Baby*, Rosemary writes the word 'Blood' on November 1st, 11/1. She then circles the 4th and 5th of October. 45 is the value of ADM (Adam). 4 + 5 = 9. Lennon was born on October 9th. Rosemary's husband points to the 4th & 5th and says 'The perfect time to make a baby.' Kubrick expressed interest in filming an adaptation of *Lord of the Rings* starring the Beatles, with Lennon as Gollum.

> *'The operations of occultism are based upon the powers of the Will and the Imagination.'* Dion Fortune

> *'The Feminine Principle conducts the work of the Imagination, while the Masculine principle conducts itself with the work of the Will.'* The Kybalion

The two tenets of Thelema are Will (Thelema) and Love. 'Do what thou wilt shall be the whole of the Law.' 'Love is the Law, Love under Will.' McCartney, with his PID mythos, represents the Will and Lennon obviously represents the IMAGINation.

In the summer of 1958, Lennon & McCartney recorded their first two songs together. That'll Be The Day That I Die, and In Spite Of All The Danger.

Are Lennon & McCartney modern day Messiahs? The archetypal death figures, resonating as the Osirian Age, signifying the advent of the Aeon of Horus?

Are they the Fools being killed by the King who refuses to relinquish the Empire?

Are they the Alephs erased from the forehead of the Golem?

Upon accepting his fate, Hamlet utters 'Let Be.'

Ob-La-Di, Ob-La-Da

SAMUEL CAMERON

This is one of the Beatles better known songs but is also one which is often despised critically for its musical and lyrical banality. Its prominence is, to some extent, due to the cover versions that have been made rather than the original. The original was not released as a single outside the UK or the USA (until 1976) but was a significant hit in some other territories. The UK hit version was by Marmalade in 1968. There have been a large number of cover versions including several by Caribbean artists. Paul McCartney has performed the song live recently. It is thus easily seen that it functions as a popularisation of the Beatles although we have to face the charge that it is, in reality, a closet McCartney solo (or even prefiguration of Wings) work. This observation fits into the common 'three phase' interpretation of the Beatles, where the final phase is the awkwardly convened collation of individual works which has been psychotherapeutically examined, in the context of the 'White Album'.

In terms of Beatles morphology, we may also note that this is essentially a love song.

Inglis has explored how the nature of Beatles love songs changed over time in line with the work of psychologist John Alan Lee, who suggests that there are six distinct styles of loving. Inglis argues that the changes reflect changes in the personal and professional lives of the individual Beatles. Change is not necessarily progress. In McCartney's case, there is more complexity, questioning and adult content in material of the Jane Asher era than there is in Ob-La-Di, Ob-La-Da. Again, it meshes with the ostensible banality of Wings' material like Silly Love Songs which is a simplistic paean to the joys of love but from a first person narrator.

In Ob-La-Di, Ob-La-Da the paean is couched in the simplistic lives and desires of an ethnic couple who are made happy by togetherness in the context of low-income and basic employment (a job on a market stall). I assume at this point that the delivery of the song is not, in any way, ironic, to which I return below.

There are two main themes worth considering in the context of this song. These are:

1) The presence of an optimistic worldview in the work of the Beatles

2) The manner of incorporation of diverse exotic or ethnic elements in the musical accompaniment.

First we must clarify a position on the issue of who is the author of the work. This song continues the tradition of crediting both Lennon and McCartney, as composers, which the latter has recently disputed. The song is only part of the body of work which might still be attributed to the Beatles as an entity due to the non-songwriting contribution of the others. However, in this specific case all the documentary evidence indicates that it is primarily a McCartney work which was violently detested by John Lennon. It was also disliked by Harrison apparently, leading to the reference to it in his Savoy Truffle. Their perceptions of it may have been influenced by the disproportionate time and effort put into it by its author but it would seem consistent to argue that they saw it as material not suitable for the collective's output. This is a persistent problem however as a jokey or light-hearted song is common with bands of this era (e.g. the Beach Boys, Byrds, Procol Harum) but these sometimes hide darker, or

even political, thinking whereas we drift here into the 'nursery rhyme' dismissal found so starkly with respect to later McCartney work.

Lennon's ire may have had an unintended positive impact as it is believed that the piano introduction, in the final version used, was rendered by him albeit in a sarcastic and dismissive manner. Despite this meaningful contribution, it is even more a McCartney work than a primary song writing authorship suggests, as it is documented that he played drums on the various versions. Note that this was a period when Ringo Starr sought to quit the band. Further, McCartney played instruments outside his basically defined group role (bass guitar) on the arrangements and Lennon's vocal and instrumental contribution to this work was small. Playing outside the defined role does not *per se* identify the song as mainly a solo work as, excepting Starr, all the Beatles tended to move between instruments as a part of the creative process.

Lennon's dislike seems to be part of a general hatred of harking back to trite singalong styles of popularity which have more in common with George Formby than the progressive stylings to which rock groups veered particularly after psychedelia and *Sgt. Pepper* (which however contained a prime specimen of McCartney vaudevillian nostalgia in When I'm Sixty-Four which was actually a song from the early Cavern days).

Ob-La-Di, Ob-La-Da continues the tradition of lightweight McCartney songs which appeared from *Sgt. Pepper* onwards which point in the direction of the overtly childlike material of the Wings era ('Mary Had A Little Lamb, Mull of Kintyre). Wings era material also features unlikely intrusions of the lightweight Caribbean stylings that occur in Ob-La-Di, Ob-La-Da into songs such as the James Bond theme Live And Let Die and the controversial Give Ireland Back To The Irish.

From a production point of view, we might argue that the genesis of Ob-La-Di, Ob-La-Da is indicative of McCartney's instinct for craftsmanship as he was seeking to master an idiom which he felt could be fruitfully embodied in his later work. In economic terms, this is product diversification which both Lennon and McCartney exhibited from early on in the range of songs they gave to others and sentimental europeanised balladry such as Michelle.

As a means of attaining wider exposure for material, we may suppose that the sing-a-long ethos and the infusion of acceptable exotic elements are acceptable strategies.

We now come to the issue of the optimistic worldview.

The lightweight Caribbean stylings help convey the optimistic worldview which was common in the diluted reggae or ska hits that has entered the British charts beginning with Millie Small's My Boy Lollipop in 1965 and later with Bob and Marcia's Young, Gifted And Black in 1970. The latter is not, in any way, ironic as it is largely a homily about how wonderful life can be rather than any kind of commentary on racial tensions. It may also be noted that calypso had become part of English culture through cricket as far back as 1950, through the victory celebration songs of Lord Kitchener and Lord Beginnner. Calypso was further embedded in British culture by the news-based observations by white comedian Lance Percival who even had a small hit in 1965 with a version of Shame And Scandal In The Family. All of these works perpetrate the idea of a mirthful and optimistic tone to Caribbean-styled music even in the face of serious or worrying events. It can be seen that this genre of work has already a worldview compatible with that often perpetuated by McCartney.

Ob-La-Di, Ob-La-Da has a very obvious optimistic perspective. The key point I want to make here is that the optimistic view in this work is specifically McCartney's rather than Lennon's. We can classify these as follows. Lennon's is utopian and universal or redemptive as in Getting Better whilst McCartney's is simplistic and quotidian. It is to be found in When I'm Sixty-Four for example although we have to note that the narrator asks if the love object will still need them when they lose hair etc. So there is scope for doubt. However, it is still relatively optimistic compared with the few other 'ageing' songs by contemporaries in this period. Pete Townshend is the obvious case but the lesser-known Ray Davies' songs Where Did My Spring Go and Shangri-La embody much more dismay about old age and are less optimistic in tone.

Lennon's optimistic worldview is to be seen in his campaigning works like Give Peace A Chance. The view in Ob-La-Di, Ob-La-Da is very explicit, as the song overtly states that the characters in the song will be happy ever after. We have to, of course, entertain the idea, of whether the song can be given an ironic treatment and thus escape the categorisation of optimistic worldview. In this regard, it is useful to make comparisons with the work of Randy Newman, which will also be helpful when we come to the exotic/ethnic elements. Love Story which was released in 1968 on his debut album has simi-lar lyrical elements to Ob-La-Di, Ob-La-Da. It is musically different as it evokes a saccharine retro American cosy family life style and builds up to a rousing chorus as opposed to Ob-La-Di, Ob-La-Da which maintains a more or less constant singalong style. The central aspects of the marriage, the ring and the house, feature in the sparse lyric. It also shares a musical setting at odds with its temporal and regional context. In this case, the sentimental orchestration harks back to a much earlier time. However, Newman's vocal and some of the string underscoring and timing of entry of parts seems to convey a strongly mocking and ironic tone despite his fairly euphoric chorus. These kinds of non-lyrical elements are not taken into account in the major statistical analysis of the 'tone' of Beatles works by Petrie et al. (2008) which claims that the Beatles' lyrics 'became darker, more psychologically distant, and less immediate over time' (ibid. p.197).

They observe that Lennon's music is usually deemed less optimistic and more melancholic than McCartney. As Lennon explained: 'He [McCartney] provided a lightness, an optimism, while I would always go for the sadness, the discords, the bluesy notes'. This is notably *not* a comment about the words as we can trade individual cases *ad infinitum* on that score, to wit Yesterday Mc-

Cartney's 'loss of mother' song is as melancholic as Lennon's Julia. In contrast, another lost mother reference song Let It Be conveys resignation but with significant optimism in the words *and* the music.

Petrie et al. (2008) use the text analysis program, *Linguistic Inquiry and Word Count* for 185 Beatles songs in three time periods: 1960–1964, 1965–1967, and 1968–1970. The data were also analysed for differences between composers in (largely) solo works and composers in combination. The estimated ANOVA showed a number of statistically significant effects. Separate linear and quadratic effects were computed. They conclude (ibid, p.200) that:

> when writing together, Lennon-McCartney produced lyrics with a highly positive emotional tone that were written predominately in the present tense. But, working mainly apart they claim that songs penned by Lennon are typically higher in negative emotion than McCartney compositions.

Most striking is that the songs by McCartney were more varied, in narrative and thematic content, compared to the other solo authors. While early songs were related to personal experiences and feelings, later songs were more often written about other people. Table 2 in this work (p.201) shows that in terms of Lennon vs McCartney comparisons, when they worked mainly jointly that positive emotions are much more present than negative. However, when working mainly apart they do not differ much (to a statistically significant degree) in the expression of positive emotions. However, Lennon's expressions of negative emotions are considerably significantly more numerous than McCartney's.

Besides not dealing with the musical background, there is also an issue with Petrie et al's categorisation of optimism vs pessimism. That is, these are seen as 'emotions' rather than a worldview. I would contend that Ob-La-Di, Ob-La-Da embodies a worldview of optimism due to the sketchy but strategic details provided on the characters which help situate their apparent happiness in a world which is intrinsically benign.

We should finally note on optimism/pessimism that there have been some general attempts (Zullow 1991) to link song contents to economic conditions but surprisingly these tend to go for the reverse causation view that the songs predict future events rather than being passively reflective of them. Like other McCartney people narrative songs, we seem to be dealing with largely a low-income economy of decent hard working people (cp. Eleanor Rigby) but, in this case, this does not dent their happiness in any way.

EXOTIC OR ETHNIC ELEMENTS

The 'foreign' elements may simply be an additional attractive element which appeals to the consumer which can be appropriated and absorbed by the host culture. This is illustrated in other pop hits like Alan Price's Don't Stop The Carnival and white calypso like Lance Percival. This has long been discussed in terms of exoticism, in the musicological literature going back to Ravel and Debussy.

We then have to come to the problem of possible accusations of racism which are a risk of ethnic and exotic divergence. This has surfaced explicitly in the context of Get Back partly enhanced by the Yoko Ono factor. However, Lennon's dislike of Ob-La-Di, Ob-La-Da is not a race issue but rather a quality one. The Beatles themselves drew on an available core of ethnically diverse music in their surrounding and early on displayed positive attitudes to ethnic musicians later extended in the sitar craze and the heavy gospel elements infused from Billy Preston in their final phase.

Their diversity focus was shown to the progenitors of the Liverpudlian ensemble, the Real Thing who had enormous hit records, in 1976 and 1979, The core members, the Amoo brothers had been active in Liverpool in the early 1960s and were even encouraged by the Beatles but to no avail. Eddy Amoo was a member of a vocal group called the Chants who met McCartney at a concert. The Chants auditioned for the Beatles who were so impressed with the group that they invited them to appear with them so they could provide the 'backing'. Brian Epstein was persuaded by John Lennon to let this occur and there was a hope that Epstein would sign them. This was a tall order, as until the emergence of the Equals in the 1960s, there was no chart presence of significantly non-white indigenous groups in the UK.

Nothing I have said serves to make this work more interesting as a song per se in terms of the music or words. However, it is an interesting prism through which to view various aspects of both the Beatles works and 'Beatlelology'.

Wild Honey Pie

MARK GOODALL

Primitivism in rock music is an essential feature of the genre, but not something readily associated with the Beatles. In fact what we are really talking about here is what Schwartz has called a 'romanticised primitivism', the myth that the more untutored a piece of music (and the musician) is the more authentic it becomes.

Texts on Wild Honey Pie, one of the Beatles' most 'primitive' songs, tend to be dismissively brief, so here I would like to accord the song a bit more time, space and consideration. The shortness of the song itself may be the source of this disparagement. You can see how after the lush ornamentation of previous Beatles recordings (notably *Sgt Pepper's Lonely Hearts Club Band*) Wild Honey Pie seems throwaway. Yet there is a lot to be said for brevity in music, especially given the horrendous self-indulgence that followed the late 1960s/early 1970s rock explosion, and if listeners find Wild Honey Pie irritating at least it only lasts for fifty-three seconds.

The form of the song, with the phrase 'Honey Pie' repeated with a single 'I love you' at the end, is basically that of a chant. This form of expression was of primary interest to the group having recently immersed themselves in Indian music (where for example the Hare Krishna — Maha Mantra — chant was essential to the development of 'Krishna Consciousness'), the incantations of Beat poet Allen Ginsberg at the First International Poetry Incarnation (held at the Royal Albert Hall in London and filmed by Peter Whitehead) and the radical outpourings of various radical political groups loudly protesting the corruption of western society such as the 'Ho Ho Ho Chi Minh' refrain shouted at pro-Communist marches (and of which Lennon would later become a staunch advocate). Admittedly Wild Honey Pie lacks the obvious sacred or political nuances of the above. Nevertheless, the song is driven by the same stripped down repetitive power that is a determining factor in popular music and the desire to affect consciousness, and is arguably an exaggeration of that repetitive phrasing characteristic of rock. In this way the song represents the primitive tendency in rock'n'roll, the artist struggling against self-imposed (musical) limitations in order to produce creative expression. The writer of Wild Honey Pie, Paul McCartney, was by now recognized as an outstanding composer and performer of songs. Yet, one is reminded of Malraux's description of the artist Henri Rousseau as being 'able to get what he wants like a child, and slightly devious with it'. The tremendous success of the Beatles' music gave them permission to play around with fragmentary *faux* naïve expressions such as this.

Musically, the song is built around elements — all performed by Paul McCartney — which seem generally to stir or to grate on the senses. These include a descending bluesy riff made up of harshly plucked acoustic guitar seventh chords, and a pounding floor tom (reminiscent of the so-called 'elderly African drum' played on an earlier tune Mr Moonlight). A wobbling slide guitar accompanies the chords. Crazed vocals with comical/disturbing voices repeat the phrases *ad nauseum*. It is the plunging and sliding dimension to Wild Honey Pie, the song taking the listener down into some hellish unknown realm that makes it so unsettling. Wild Honey Pie is a jam that starts and ends nowhere in particular, the reversal of the pleasant and vivid location-setting of songs such as Eleanor Rigby, Penny Lane and Strawberry Fields Forever. It is also the sound of someone staggering drunk/stoned with trembling legs down a moving, shifting passageway. The associations with repetition made by music critics usually come with negative insinuations relating to a perceived loss of subjectivity in a primitive or hypnotic state. Yet, these elements are also what characterize the pleasure of pop and rock music. The limitations of trance-like tunes such as Wild Honey Pie create a news sense of subversive experience.

As well as being concise, Wild Honey Pie holds the distinction of being perhaps the most hated song on the 'White Album'. Both ends of the critical spectrum, from serious to frivolous, have been scathing. Ian MacDonald in *Revolution in the Head* dismisses it in one sentence and David Quantick in his book *Revolution* describes it as 'hellish'. When George Martin famously declared of the 'White Album' that he 'didn't think that a lot of the songs were worthy of release' he was undoubtedly thinking of fragments such as this. In the era of the orderly classic rock LP it would have seemed indulgent to intersperse full-length songs (of which there are many on the 'White Album') with scraps of unfinished improvisations. Nowadays, with the proliferation of extended CD releases, with bonus recordings, alternative mixes and demos, housed in very expansive (and expensive) packaging, the Beatles were perhaps simply prefiguring the completist obsessions of the twentieth century audiences?

The other point critics of the song fail to observe is that Wild Honey Pie is designed to be listened to in the context of the tracks that both precede and follow it. The derided repetition of the track is 'ruptured' by the things that appear either side of it: the somewhat predictable crash ending of Ob-La-Di, Ob-La-Da and on the other side the fast Spanish guitar intro to The Continuing Story of Bungalow Bill. Sandwiched between these two disparate musical moments, with the intersection of these elements when taken as a sequence profound, it is arguable that Wild Honey Pie makes more sense. To paraphrase Chateaubriand, it is sometimes the little details rather than the grandiose ideas that go straight to the heart.

The Beatles were now in a position to do as they pleased. 'Let's offer our fans a song dump of everything we have thought up in the last year; why be selective and restrained? They can have it warts and all' the group seem to be stating with this practice, and Wild Honey Pie is the contribution that seems to epitomise this more than any other.

The realm of rock repetition easily copes with the experience of sameness.

Richard Meltzer, *The Aesthetics of Rock*

The Continuing Story of Bungalow Bill

MARK GOODALL

One can view The Continuing Story Of Bungalow Bill as a droll companion piece to Happiness Is A Warm Gun, a less harrowing work typical of Lennon's more humorous and surreal perspectives on contemporaneous subjects and themes. Seymour Chwast's bizarre illustration for the song printed in Alan Aldridge's *The Beatles Illustrated Lyrics* book sets the tone perfectly, a kind of dark but silly tableaux that could have come straight from the *Yellow Submarine* film. Chwast at one time specialized in graphic illustrations replete with social commentary, a poster such as his classic 'END BAD BREATH' anti-Vietnam protest work symbolizing the same caustic yet funny expression Lennon was himself keen on. Like Happiness Is A Warm Gun, The Continuing Story Of Bungalow Bill is a pointed critique of American gun laws and the casual and habitual use of violence in Western culture. This is accentuated in the Chwast graphic for the song where a big-game hunter sits atop an elephant brandishing a rifle and dressed in Confederate clobber (instead of safari gear) — the 'all-American bullet-headed Saxon mother's son' of the song's lyric. An already bagged tiger is draped across the back of the elephant while another victim peers out of the bush. In *Revolution in the Head* Ian Macdonald remarks on how the song was inspired by the seeming hypocrisy of an American student who had joined the Beatles and the Maharishi Mahesh Yogi at Rishikesh but who departed for a few weeks of tiger hunting in between bouts of spiritual fulfilment. This is true, but what seems like absurd double standards to European eyes is more likely indicative of how deeply embedded firearms, hunting and shooting are in the American psyche (see Happiness Is A Warm Gun) so that personal spiritual enlightenment and animal welfare can be completely exclusive. Aside from the disturbing Americana of the

lyrics, the song appears to draw inspiration too from the British colonial experience in Africa and India (where of course Rishikesh is located) and the infamous grotesque black and white photographs of mountains of wildlife exterminated by the numerous Britannic personifications of Bungalow Bill (also parodied by The Bonzo Dog Doo Dah Band in Hunting Tigers Out In Indiah), appalling images which British schoolchildren of the postwar era were familiar with.

Recorded very quickly, with typical Lennon impatience, in three takes, the song has a ramshackle feel to it, hardly developed much from the Esher/'Kinfauns' demo version that has since been widely circulated. Macdonald chides the results as 'tub-thumping banality' but I must admit to feeling sympathy with Lennon's rushed style of recording. Musicians will know that there is an inordinate amount of time (and money) wasted in the recording studio faffing around with endless effects, complicated recording techniques and long-winded set ups by which time you have lost all the spontaneous energy, enthusiasm and drive of the original creative spark. Some of the recordings on the 'White Album' were indubitably recorded in this manner as a deliberate contrast with the long sessions for *Sgt Pepper.*

'The Continuing Story Of Bungalow Bill' switches between major and minor keys for the verse and oscillates between fast and slow sections between verse and chorus. An intriguing and incredibly speedy scale run on a Spanish guitar opens the song. For a long time I pondered over which Beatle played this complicated bit of guitar virtuosity before deciding it must be George. Later I found out that it was of course dubbed on afterwards probably from another non-Beatle source. More sneaky trickery…

The unmistakable voice of Yoko Ono can be heard singing the line 'not when he looked so fierce', a hint, for some a warning, of the collaborations between her and Lennon soon to bear fruit.

While My Guitar Gently Weeps

TONY KEEN

1967 wasn't a particularly good year for George Harrison. The creation of *Sgt. Pepper's Lonely Hearts Club Band* and *Magical Mystery Tour* centred on Paul McCartney and John Lennon developing songs in the studio, while Harrison and Ringo Starr sat around waiting to play. At least Starr knew he would, for most tracks, eventually be called upon. But solos in 1967 were often not played on guitar, but on piano, or even on piccolo trumpet or cut-up tape loops of fairground organs and calliopes. When there was a guitar solo, it might not be played by Harrison, but by Lennon or McCartney. Sometimes, a Harrison solo might be replaced by one by McCartney, if Paul didn't think George was getting it just right, a practice that dated back to 1965. On one of the Beatles' most iconic tracks, A Day In The Life, Harrison's sole contribution was to shake maracas.

Ironically, the marginalization of Harrison as a guitarist in the Beatles coincided with a general increase in the status of the guitarist in pop music. In the 1950s and early 1960s, with a few exceptions the focus had been on singers. The guitarist became more important with Keith Richards in the Rolling Stones, followed by Eric Clapton in John

Mayall's Bluesbreakers and Cream, Clapton's replacement in The Yardbirds, Jeff Beck, and Pete Townshend of The Who. At the end of 1966 and beginning of 1967 all these were eclipsed by Jimi Hendrix.

Though it's sometimes easy to imagine the Beatles as aloof from other developments in 1960s pop, of course they weren't. Harrison knew about the growing wave of guitar heroes. Clapton was Harrison's extra-Beatle friend, in the same way that Barry Miles, John Dunbar and the Indica crowd were for McCartney and Yoko Ono was just becoming for Lennon. And Harrison was at early gigs by Hendrix.

Harrison may well have wondered why he wasn't accorded the same status. He still wasn't even after the Beatles broke up, because he wasn't that sort of guitarist. In place of Clapton or Townshend's flashy showmanship, Harrison was, like Starr, and to a lesser extent McCartney, an economic musician, only playing what a song needed, and no more. Long, self-indulgent solos were never his thing.

At the same time as being marginalized as a musician, he was also being marginalized as a songwriter. Harrison was, if Bill Harry's story about the creation of Don't Bother Me is to be believed, a reluctant composer, and indeed after that track on *With The Beatles* he produced nothing worth recording for eighteen months. But he had two tracks on *Help!* and *Rubber Soul* and three on *Revolver*. For *Pepper* he was cut back to just one, Within You, Without You. His other potential contribution, Only A Northern Song, bitterly mocking the 'Northern childhood' concept originally behind *Pepper*, was hidden away in the soundtrack to the movie *Yellow Submarine*. The same fate befell It's All Too Much, an overlong Harrison-style approach to the same ideas as Lennon's simultaneously-composed All You Need Is Love. He did get a track on *Magical Mystery Tour*, but it is the nadir of his compositions as a Beatle, Blue Jay Way, a song that is never able to escape the boredom out of which it was written.

1968 must have seemed rather brighter. Recording Hey Bulldog signalled the Beatles' return to sounding more like a rock'n'roll band than they had for a year, which should lead to more of a role for Harrison as a lead guitarist. He also composed and produced the soundtrack album for *Wonderwall Music*, the first official solo release for a Beatle; out of this came The Inner Light, which went on the B-side of Lady Madonna, Harrison's first composing credit on a single.

That said, his actual songwriting contributions to the 'White Album' aren't that impressive. Leaving aside for a moment While My Guitar

Gently Weeps, Piggies is just nasty, Savoy Truffle rocks along inconsequentially, with a lyric every bit as penetrating as expected from a song about chocolates, and Long, Long, Long shares far too much with Bob Dylan's Sad Eyed Lady Of The Lowlands, being an early example of the plagiaristic tendencies that would get Harrison in trouble over My Sweet Lord. Three more songs were demoed at the end of May 1968 at Kinfauns, his Esher home. Of these, Circles is a dreary dirge. Not Guilty, another song complaining about how Lennon and McCartney treated him, was tried in the studio, but ultimately abandoned as Harrison clearly couldn't quite get what he wanted. Perhaps the best of these is Sour Milk Sea, the only one that saw the light of day in 1968, being given to Apple artist Jackie Lomax. As this version was produced by Harrison, and features McCartney and Starr, as well as Clapton and pianist Nicky Hopkins, it's safe to assume that any Beatles version would have sounded similar. But it doesn't quite sound right for the Beatles, having more in common with Clapton's early solo work.

Taken as a group, what all these songs suggest is that Harrison, whose material previously fitted comfortably with Lennon and McCartney's work, was now moving in a different direction, towards a heavier sound. This made perfect sense in the context of the 'White Album', where Lennon and McCartney were also moving away from each other. And if Harrison's attempts at a heavier idiom are less successful than Lennon's in the single version of Revolution, they are at least less risible than McCartney's Helter Skelter.

While My Guitar Gently Weeps was first demoed on acoustic guitar at Kinfauns, and then recorded in the studio on 25 July 1968, again on acoustic guitar, with a harmonium accompaniment that Mark Lewisohn attributes to McCartney, but could well be Harrison himself. When released on *Anthology 3*, this version garnered much praise, and formed the basis of the version on *LOVE*. But it's unlikely that Harrison intended this as more than another demo. He probably always intended a weeping guitar effect to match the lyrics. The various recordings allow the evolution of the song to be traced, as Harrison discarded several verses. Walter Everitt expresses surprise that the line 'I look at the floor and I see it needs sweeping' survived this, but it's key to the song's effect. Like Within You, Without You, While My Guitar Gently Weeps is a song expressing sadness at all the people who cannot open themselves up to the totality of human experience ('love') — but this line shows that the narrator himself is as unable to escape mundanity as those he comments on.

The full band version of While My Guitar Gently Weeps was begun on 16 August. Harrison then spent 2 September trying to get a backwards guitar solo to his satisfaction, before deciding to start again on 5 September. But Harrison wasn't impressed with the lack of effort being put in by Lennon and McCartney.

Through much of the 'White Album' sessions, Harrison was struggling towards Clapton-style guitar solos, sometimes successfully, as on Yer Blues, sometimes not quite getting there, as on Not Guilty, and, a little less short of the mark, Savoy Truffle. When producing the Lomax version of Sour Milk Sea, Harrison's answer to the question 'What would Eric Clapton play?' had been to invite Clapton himself to provide the solo. On 6 September, he decided this was also the solution to the problems he was having on While My Guitar Gently Weeps. Clapton was very reluctant, protesting that other people didn't play on Beatles records. Of course, they did, and had done since George Martin added piano on the *Please Please Me* sessions. But Martin, and other people who played occasional keyboards such as Mal Evans, were, until Nicky Hopkins played on Revolution a couple of months earlier, Beatles insiders. Outsiders did play on Beatles tracks, ever since John Scott had added flutes to You've Got To Hide Your Love Away in 1965, but on instruments the Beatles did not play. Guitars were only played by Harrison, Lennon or McCartney, unless the rumours that Carl Perkins played on their version of his song Matchbox are to be believed. In this the Beatles were more rigid than some of their rivals: The Rolling Stones had long employed session musicians, in particular Hopkins, and had started to record with whoever turned up in the studio on a given day, accredited member of the band or not. Brian Wilson had largely stopped using the Beach Boys as musicians in 1966.

In any case, Harrison was adamant; he wanted Clapton. The immediate effect of Clapton's presence, aside from getting Harrison the effect he wanted, was that it got McCartney to behave and take the track seriously. Harrison remembered this a few months later, when he invited Billy Preston to play in the *Get Back* sessions as a means of putting his bandmates on their best behaviour.

Looking at Lennon's contribution to the track is instructive. Harrison worked very hard on Lennon's tracks, in particular Yer Blues. Lennon did not reciprocate. He played organ on the first band version, and guitar on the second, but his contribution was such that it was essentially wiped, and survives only in brief notes in the outro. He seems not to have been present at the final session with Clapton, though in the final mixing session he did add ''ey up!' at the end of The Continuing Story Of Bungalow Bill to lead into While My Guitar Gently Weeps, rather undermining it. On Piggies he only suggested one of the nastier lines and put together pig effects from tape loops and his own voice. He very likely played electric piano on early takes of Not Guilty, but it's less clear that he played the harpsichord that replaced the piano. It certainly doesn't sound much like Lennon, and Harrison, McCartney and Chris Thomas have all been suggested. Most accounts agree that Lennon did not play on Savoy Truffle, and all that he played no part in Long, Long, Long.

Lennon was going through a very selfish phase in 1968. He wanted to be at the centre of everything, hence his desire to have Yoko Ono by his side all the time, and his resentment at McCartney making tracks on his own. But there was little reciprocity.

Compare this with McCartney. McCartney was bossy, and unable to treat Harrison as a grown adult — but he turned up to do the work. He made three important contributions to While My Guitar Gently Weeps, once he started taking the song seriously. Firstly, there's his piano opening, which sets exactly the right mournful note for the song. Then there is his thumping bass, played on his new Fender Jazz, and possibly thickened and given edge either by guitar or by the Fender Bass VI, a six-stringed bass played by Harrison on the Hey Jude film clip, and much used by Lennon and Harrison in the Get Back sessions. Finally, his descant vocals contribute significantly to Harrison's double-tracked voice on the later verses.

Critical reaction to While My Guitar Gently Weeps has been mixed. Ian MacDonald found it 'tiresome', and to Sean Egan it is the weakest of Harrison's tracks on The Beatles. But this is not the popular consensus. While My Guitar Gently Weeps is the earliest Harrison track to warrant a place in the red and blue compilations of 1973, and remained a part of Harrison's live set after the Beatles split. It is often played in tribute to Harrison, most notably at his posthumous 2004 induction into the Rock & Roll Hall of Fame, with a blistering guitar solo by Prince. It foreshadows a much better 1969 for Harrison, with his second B-side, Old Brown Shoe, as good a B-side as the band ever hand, and his contributions to Abbey Road, Something and Here Comes The Sun, clearly both superior to anything Lennon or McCartney wrote for that album.

Happiness is a Warm Gun

MARK GOODALL

'I think he showed me the cover of a magazine that said, "Happiness is a warm gun." It was a gun magazine, that's it: I read it, thought it was a fantastic, insane thing to say. A warm gun means you've just shot something.'

John Lennon, *Lennon Remembers*

'I think this is my favourite on The Beatles album.'

Paul McCartney, *The Beatles Illustrated Lyrics*

In retrospect, the above lines, uttered by John Lennon in December 1970, appear tragically prophetic. Inspired by an article entitled Happiness Is A Warm Gun in *American Rifleman* (May 1968), Lennon used the phrase to concoct a spirited attack on the conflation of violence and sexuality in the American psyche. The insanity of the phrase is all the more telling as such a philosophy is perverse expressed in a popular magazine. Warren W. Herlihy, the author of the article, rhapsodises about the day he bought his seven-year-old son John his first gun (a Remington Model 514) which, as it came of the box, is described as 'a real sweetheart'. The key phrase for designating the subsequent father/son killing spree, stretching out over some years and taking in many 'kills', was 'happiness' (the picture in the article shows John posing with his death tools). It was this that Lennon no doubt, like any peace-loving individual, found perverse. Moreover, the conflation of 'romance' with 'violence' in the piece similarly is shocking.

Firearms also loom large in the pantheon of rock mythology. My first personal encounter with popular music and guns was catching Sid Vicious' performance of My Way on TV, where, at the end of a sneering performance of the song, he turns his pistol on to the audience (this was filmed at the Olympia theatre in Paris, which hideously came to mind in a strange kind of reversal with the terrorist massacres at another Parisian music venue the Bataclan in December 2015). Then there was the discovery of the deaths by shooting of Sam Cooke, Marvin Gaye, Felix Pappalardi and of course Lennon himself. Guns wielded in popular music mean crime (Miss Otis Regrets, Whisky In The Jar, I Shot The Sheriff), suicide (Le Poinçonneur Des Lilas and Quand Mon 6.35 Me Fait Les Yeux Doux by Serge Gainsbourg), murder (Hey Joe), revolution (Guns Of Brixton and 1977 by The Clash), state control (Bullet In The Head by Rage Against the Machine) and paranoia (Shot by Both Sides by Magazine). The myth of the rock star as a swaggering gun-toting outlaw, perhaps best personified by the image constructed by American musicians such as The Eagles (see the cover of *Desperado*) and Ted Nugent, continues to this day through the language both visual and aural of rap and hip hop. It's obvious listening to Happiness Is A Warm Gun that Lennon, though a tough guy in his early years, was reacting against such machismo.

The song is a nice distillation of Lennon's sweeping obsessions and his own musical and personal trajectory. The song points towards his upcoming solo career with its mix of experimental rock, folk and a retreat always into rock and roll nostalgia. One of the aspects of the Beatles work that is satisfying is their ability to introduce humour (of a particularly black and surreal kind) into their songs — even the most serious seeming ones. The final section of the song in particular acts as both an exquisite rendering out

of, and mockery of, their roots in American popular music.

The final lyrics about 'holding you like a gun' (echoed in the superb postpunk Nietzschean classic She Is Beyond Good And Evil by The Pop Group) do certainly contain the sexual dimension, as many commentators have observed, but they are also a critical and ironic comment on the American obsession with the right to bear arms and its inevitable violent conclusion. Happiness Is A Warm Gun is also a taster for the savage political and social commentary that would make up much of Lennon's future solo musical output.

Common wisdom is that the song comprises of three previous incomplete Lennon songs. However, in the finished version there are actually four or even five sections. In terms of construction, the song, like A Day In A Life disproves the common assumption that sticking random bits of songs together betrays a lack of ideas. Few bands can pull this trick off effectively (critics have referenced the Incredible String Band in this context and Radiohead arguably managed it with Paranoid Android).

A dreamy opening finger-picked section on a flanged electric guitar; a plodding section; a waltz featuring a fuzz-guitar; the 'mother-su-

Fig.2
The
American
Rifleman
May 1968

HAPPINESS IS A WARM GUN

Primer popping with pop from early boyhood

By WARREN W. HERLIHY

IN my gun cabinet two "little guns" I have a special place of honor. One is a Remington Model 514 single-shot .22; the other, a Winchester Model 37 boy's 20 ga. shotgun.

The bores are clean and the barrels have a good bit of their original bluing. Sometimes I open the cabinet to admire their polished stocks and well-oiled metal. They bring back memories.

I remember a little boy, my son, now a strapping man of 18, and his joy when he got his first gun. I remember those grand times we had over the years, father and son, each as enthusiastic about guns as the other.

It is hard to believe, that it was 11 years ago when I was getting ready to go off on a Sunday afternoon for a few hours shooting with some buddies.

I was on the way to the car, loaded down with guns, shooting mat, the works, when a little voice said, "Dad, take me."

It was son John, then all of 7 years old. I pondered a moment: sure, he was young, but—off we went. And what a time we had that Sunday. I let him shoot an M1 carbine. The stock was short, the recoil mild, and John enjoyed every shot he cranked off.

Lots of shooting

He was hooked, no doubt about it. So we went off to a nearby quarry and shot, shot, shot for the next few months. He loved shooting, and had so much fun that there was only one thing to do: get him a gun of his own.

I decided on a Remington Model 514, the one that's still in my cabinet. It was a real sweetheart just as it came out of the box, but I thought John would have better luck with it if a few modifications were made.

The stock was shortened to fit John, the trigger smoothed up and adjusted for a 3-lb. pull, and a Lyman receiver sight and a Redfield front sight with interchangeable elements were mounted. Finally, we fitted it with a small sling.

The day it was ready we took off for the quarry, loaded down with ammo. John got the feel of the little Reming-

ton right off and in no time flat he was putting round after round into the black at 50 yds.

We banged away in the quarry for a few weeks until it was quite clear John was ready for a hunt up Crow Canyon for squirrels. That was real shooting. Warm sun, big, puffy clouds chasing across the sky, and all the squirrels anyone could ask for.

John really had the bug. Every weekend it was the same story. "Let's go shooting, Dad." And, since I sort of like to shoot myself, we went.

By the time he was 8, I figured John was ready for a shotgun. But how much recoil could he take? What gauge would be best? That's where shooting friends come in. After lots of jaw-boning with gunsmiths, sporting goods store owners and shotgunners, I decided on a Winchester Model 37. With its short stock, recoil pad and swell workmanship, the 20-ga. was a real rugged field gun, just the thing to start a lad off with.

Clay bird practice

Long and hard we practiced. I'd throw the clay birds by hand, John would try to knock them down. Once he could hit the clay birds more times than not, it was off to the local trap range. I'll tell you, it did me a world of good to watch John work that little Winchester. Pretty soon he was popping the discs while I was missing them.

It was fall before we knew it, and time for pheasant hunting. Opening day of the season we tried our luck. Poor old dad missed his chances, but not John. He connected with a big rooster with long spurs, flushed by his dog, Happy.

The years went by. Happy years. Hunting ducks and geese in mud up to the arm pits, rain streaming down our necks. Through those years that kid of mine made kills that would turn a veteran shotgunner blue—not with cold but with envy.

Soon John was old enough to take the NRA Hunter Safety course. Maybe he did know a good bit about guns and safety, but it was a chance to let him hear it from someone else. It's a fine course and he learned a lot from a good instructor.

Boys have a way of growing up. And one day, just before bird season, John announced that the 20-ga. was too small. Now he wanted a "big" gun.

We shopped around, checking out weight, stock fit, swing, action. We set-

The Herlihys ate pheasant after young John's first wildfowl hunt.

tled for a pump gun, a Hi-Standard 12-ga. Model 200 with ventilated rib. It suited John to a tee. He got his limit with it that year and has done real well with it ever since.

John has other "big" guns now. For rifles he has a fine old .30-30 Winchester Model 94 and a Remington Model 700 with a 6X Weaver scope. He handles them like a man, which is natural because he is a man now.

But we still keep those "little" guns because they stand for something. To me, they stand for the comradeship and good times a father and son can have when they share a love of guns and shooting. I'm never sorry I gave in when John pleaded, "Take me, Dad." ∎

perior jump the gun' section in 6/8 time; and the doo-wop finale. Time signatures change rapidly throughout the song disconcerting the listener, pulling the listener through some strange kind of journey. The song features one of Lennon's best vocal performances, starting softly before becoming more remote and bluesy, ending in a raw yet sweet high-noted climax, all demonstrating his skill at switching between moods within a few short seconds. The sweet backing vocals hark back to early Beatles harmonies and are either an effective accompaniment to the instrumentation (as it usually was back then) or a parody (or, as is also often the case with the Beatles, both).

Happiness Is A Warm Gun is one of the most striking songs on the 'White Album' and its place in the Beatles complete works still stands in the twenty-first century as unique and powerful.

Martha My Dear

DAVID KANE

Saturday, 5th October 1968

He was stirred from his slumber: a familiar noise had worked its way into his dreams. It was so familiar in fact that his rest was not entirely disrupted. Instead, he found himself an inhabitant of the curious no man's land between sleep and consciousness, the slow moving river that invites you to float downstream for hours, observing the past and the present in gentle collision. Remnants drifted before him, the familiar faces; the graceful arc of the swallow's dive, the frogs suspended on a barbed wire fence that horrified little Michael. His childhood handiwork, preparation for a fight that did not materialize and overtaken by preparation for the life he was destined to lead.

Mother Mary, cycling off in the snow to attend another's birth, always doing her best for her own family and for everyone else. What would she think of all this? There she is, a shadow moving past the bedroom door and now, not even a shadow. How are we going to get by without her money? Dad

Jim, playing the piano and demonstrating harmony, giving him a head start — always ahead of the pack, always knowing that little bit more. His own early forays into composition; standing at the same piano, picking out a tune, working in the key of C. Half a song, an original song that would be utilized later. Borrowed from dad's old time numbers and family party pieces, the past channeled towards the future. A fulsome sack of ideas that could be rummaged through at will and turned into something new.

Always an observer he watched, often from the top deck of the bus, alone. Seeing and imagining — waiting for it all to begin. Gathering material, living the life he imagined an artist would lead. Travelling the streets of Speke and Allerton, completely certain of his destination: how could it be anything else? This was his time: Lonnie, Elvis, Buddy, Gene and Little Richard Penniman, trapped inside and occasionally bursting free. Talking endlessly about rock and roll; and, when not talking about it, playing it on piano and guitar. Devouring every new release, memorizing the words and painstakingly working out the guitar parts. These were his new lessons, ones that replaced formal schooling. This was his education; this was going to get him where he wanted to be. American rock and roll had swept away the grey clouds that hung over the postwar 'Pool. Tom Ewell's call for colour and a wider screen in the opening moments of The Girl Can't Help It signalled a fundamental change taking place and corresponded with his own broadening teenage horizons: he had the confidence and the talent — what could stop him?

The metallic threads of his white sports coat sparkled in the summer sun. He mingled with the crowd at the fête, keeping an eye on the girls who were keeping an eye on him. Entering into the coolness of the church hall with single-minded purpose — to make an impression, to show what he could do. He did it well; he was better than them — he knew it. He could sing better than Sinatra. He could outplay them all, picking up their instruments and quickly outstripping them. It was simply a question of time; a matter of finding the right blend. Finding the right personnel who understood what the pecking order was, who knew their place.

White turned to black, black leather and he was in another country, picking up a different set of skills. Gangsters, spivs, chancers, sailors and shy existentialists became their audience and test bed — this was a coming of age. A harsh, guttural voice implored them to 'Mach Schau! Mach Schau!' And Mach Shau they did, on and off stage, learning, storing it away. It was their job to generate the beat, as murderous as a spring-loaded truncheon and as irresistible as the working girls that befriended and indulged them. Staying awake for days without the chemical assistance favoured by the others — always a little careful: taking it all in, banking it for later use. Switching to bass, the instrument that was in his genes — it was meant to be. They were an unstoppable force.

A jet-engine roar swept overhead, drowning out the gentle burble of the water; it enveloped him, cut him off. The pin sharp faces dissolved into a blur and easily recalled conversations gave way to hissing white noise. Everything began to get faster, began to swirl. John swept by in a reverie, unaware of his surroundings. There was a time when they had faced each other, eyeball to eyeball and worked as a team, learning their craft, inking proudly proclaimed originals. When what they craved was delivered, it could not be sustained. Time became their enemy; deadlines, schedules. There is no time like the present and yet the present gives us no time. Seated at a table; feeling stifled by this tedious business. The long days of endless conversations with armies of suits, porcine suits with their snouts in the trough that he had bought and filled, far removed from the business of making music, the real business — our business.

He realized that his world had changed and so, inevitably, had people. The sentimental side of his personality momentarily got the better of him; he longed for the simpler times; he still needed a nod of approval from his friend; the mutual recognition of each other's talents that had bound them together from their first meeting. He felt an irritation, an itch accompanied by a rise in temperature. John was moving further away and not looking back, he had weighed anchor. He felt a flush of anger at his friend's selfishness then calmed. John had always been this way — it was always John first. He knew it was his responsibility to hold this together. But who is my anchor? A wave of panic broke over him. He needed a presence — someone to keep him grounded, who reminded him of family, someone to share all of this with. He needed his own rock: one that wouldn't smash him to smithereens on contact.

The mechanical assault was replaced by music, which gradually grew in intensity; at first it seemed unworldly, different to his ears. He became attuned to the sound, Eastern stringed instruments, rapid, powerful percussion. It filled his senses, overwhelming his stately progress. He made a conscious effort to close his mind to the tumult surrounding him and focused on a figure in the distance, elegant, immaculate, just as I remember him and now, he's gone. Another who left too soon replaced, temporarily, with a smiling, giggling charlatan who promised much but ultimately failed to deliver. Jane, also gone: he suddenly felt quite alone. He missed her. They couldn't find the right words for each other. His words were reserved for a different purpose and often, everything else came a poor second to his primary goal — his compulsion. All these people leaving, moving away: he needed someone to move towards him, someone who would stay.

He shook himself free from the negativity: his instinctiveness would guide him — it hadn't let him down yet. It was, however, necessary to concentrate, to keep focused, to keep learning. Soak it all up; every experience was something to be used. He was willing, he was always eager and keen to please and be praised. His diligence was often rewarded, plucked from a conveyor belt of ideas; not tortured, not wrenched from his soul, but crafted. He was a master craftsman, at the top of his game. He had forgotten or rejected more than some would produce in their lifetime; he was number one. He longed for the darkness of the studio in the small hours when it all came together. When the ideas coalesced into something tangible. This was his domain, his kingdom. When the others had lost interest and were long gone, he

was still there, changing, improving, shaping. This was where the acid tongues were silenced and he indulged himself, fed his desire for perfection. This is for me and mine. Who needs them? I am the band; I am the composer and the orchestra.

A familiar tune played and he was seated at the piano. He was working on an exercise, a motif; something that was perhaps slightly beyond his capabilities but he was determined to master it. John had unwittingly inspired him, piqued his competitive nature. He mouthed some sounds, something to fit. Let it go where it wants to go. In his mind, an arrangement formed and with a familiar flush of excitement, he was heading down a path well trodden. It fell into place, quickly and easily. He hummed it for George; George will take care of it. He was a skilled interpreter and would recruit the personnel required to colour in the initial sketches and make it whole. They worked long into the morning, painting pictures with sound. The initial brush strokes were augmented, fleshed out and finished with a flourish. The result was a picture to be displayed and admired.

It was ceaseless; his constant companion; his closest friend and confidant. The one thing he could rely on. The snatches of rhythm and rhyme that might, once upon a time,

Fig.3
Paul McCartney
and Martha
© Barry Henson

have been someone else's but now, were his. Reaching once again into the sack of ideas: family, friends, Liverpool, rock and roll. The sights and sounds that fed his gift; the noises of the city, instruments, chance encounters, snatched conversations, newspaper stories and a dog's plaintive bark. The latter grew in volume as he coasted into the shallows of the river before gently bumping ashore.

What time is it? He blinked and noticed light streaming through the curtained window. Ok, that's good — it isn't the middle of the night at least. The memories of yesterday returned: the satisfaction of a job well done, another one in the can; another deadline met.

The rhythmic racket — the canine cacophony — continued, holding a steady beat. He patted his palm on the bedclothes in time. Then, he was up, swinging his legs out of bed and landing firmly at the beginning of a new day — another day.

'Hang on a sec Martha, I haven't forgotten about you… no one is ever going to forget about you.'

Additional Sources

Lewisohn, M. *The Beatles — All These Years. Volume 1: Tune In*. London: Little, Brown, 2013.

Lewisohn, M. *The Complete Beatles Chronicles*. London: Pyramid, 1992.

MacDonald, I. *Revolution in the Head*. London: Pimlico, 1998.

Miles, B. *Paul McCartney: Many Years From Now*. London: Vintage, 1998.

I'm So Tired

BECCY OWEN

I was listening to this song recently in a twenty-four-hour supermarket at 4am. As I shuffled alongside all the other sleepless folk, I found myself smiling wryly at John's empathic lyrics.

For most of my life I've been an insomniac. I've always got to sleep fine, but I wake up an hour or so later and then that's often me. Ping! For hours. Sometimes the rest of the night. I've made records, crocheted whole blankets, gone for a run, all in the middle of the night as an alternative to lying there, inert.

I read once that sleep deprivation is something that accumulates over time and is impossible to claw back. You'd have to hibernate for a season to make up the lost shuteye. I'm yet to find a suitable cave and still, life goes on. And on.

This year I was diagnosed with Bipolar II and I've being doing a lot of work around triggers, symptoms and wellness strategies.

Turns out that an intermittent sleep pattern can be a symptom of the illness for many people. Also turns out that an intermittent sleep pattern can be a powerful trigger for a depressive or hypermanic episode. The cruelty of this kind of catch-22 is well-known to people who find getting or staying asleep hard: you're desperate to get enough but you're so wrapped up in the fear that you might not get enough that you're very likely to end up in fact not getting enough sleep. Maybe it's like sex: the more desperate you are for it, the less likely you are to get any.

John Lennon was bang on when he sang 'it's no joke, I'm going insane.' And in many ways, the bipolarity of this song — the shift from hang-dog, country lullaby to disgruntled rock'n'roll tantrum — feels incredibly apt when you're still in the reduced aisle buying a 20p pasty for breakfast as the sun starts to rise.

Blackbird

GREG WILSON

Black culture is central to the story of the Beatles, their love of Rock & Roll and Rhythm & Blues the driving force behind their rise to the pop music summit.

I remember having a conversation once with a guy who was big into the Northern Soul scene at its seventies heights. I learnt that his appreciation of Soul had come via the Beatles — the 1963 albums, *Please Please Me* and *With The Beatles* having come into his home via an older sibling. He loved what he heard, but he also read the sleeve credits and, having worked out the names Lennon & McCartney as band members who'd written some of the tracks, wondered who the other writers were, eventually discovering that a number of these inclusions were cover versions of records by black American artists — Arthur Alexander, The Cookies, The Shirelles (two tracks), The Isley Brothers, The Marvelettes, Chuck Berry, The Miracles, The Donays and Barrett Strong all represented on those first two Beatles LPs. Taking into account that the originals weren't to be found in the British Hit Parade, the Beatles clearly had a deeper than surface appreciation of black music.

All this tells us that, despite growing up in an environment of open racism, these four Liverpudlians had somehow risen above this to take their place at the vanguard of a youth movement steeped in black music — for it wasn't just the Beatles, but Liverpool musicians in general who embraced the authenticity of these remarkable recordings from America, which seeped raw emotion. In *The Best Of Fellas* (2002), Merseybeat historian Spencer Lee's book about former Cavern DJ, Bob Wooler, there's a fascinating chapter where Wooler and Lee look at every song that was covered and recorded by the groups in Liverpool during this period — the

cut off point being the release of the *Sgt. Pepper's Lonely Hearts Club Band* album in 1967. It's a compelling illustration of just how reliant the Merseybeat groups were on black American music.

With over 350 cover versions listed, black American artists were overwhelmingly in the majority, with a whopping 60% of the total, significantly more than their white counterparts. This domination is further outlined via the fact that eight of the top ten artists covered were black — Chuck Berry, Little Richard, The Drifters, Larry Williams, The Coasters, Ray Charles, Arthur Alexander and The Shirelles (the white artists being Carl Perkins and The Everly Brothers).

Whilst black American music was the prime source of inspiration, there were black musicians from the Beatles' home city with whom they crossed-paths, picked up ideas from and even collaborated with — Liverpool's black community being Britain's oldest, dating back to the 1700s.

The Chants who, as far as the Merseybeat scene is concerned, might be described as the one that got away, were very much held back by the fact that they were black. Their best-known recording was their first, 1963's I Could Write A Book, written by Rodgers &

Hart, which originally appeared in the 1940 musical *Pal Joey* and was later made into a 1957 movie where it was sung by Frank Sinatra. It was given the thumbs up by all four Beatles during their appearance as judges on the British TV show *Juke Box Jury*, although even the Fabs' wholehearted endorsement failed to help it break into the charts.

Whilst lesser Merseybeat lights had their fifteen minutes in the national spotlight, The Chants would, unfortunately, never have a hit single — despite releasing records through the sixties and into the seventies. They just never got the breaks they needed, even with support from the Beatles and, for a period, having Brian Epstein manage them. Founder member Eddie Amoo would hook-up with younger brother Chris in the mid-seventies — their band, The Real Thing, going on to achieve international success.

It wasn't in Liverpool where the Beatles first connected with The Chants, but in nearby New Brighton, where the Beatles were supporting US icon Little Richard at The Tower Ballroom (October 12th 1962), their first single, Love Me Do, having entered the chart that very week.

Bill Harry, founder of *Merseybeat*, wrote about Chant Joey Ankrah's exchange with Beatle Paul McCartney on the night.

'He "blagged" his way into Little Richard's dressing room after the concert and Paul spotted him leaving. Paul wanted to find out who he was and was fascinated when Joe told him about being in an a cappella group. He then gave Joe a note, signed by himself, for the Chants to produce at the Cavern when the Beatles returned from Hamburg. They did this, turning up for one of the lunchtime sessions. They waited for the Beatles to come off stage and "waylaid" them when they left the dressing room as the gig emptied. Paul introduced them to the rest of the group and then beckoned them onto the stage.'

Eddie Amoo recalls:

'They went "apeshit" when we started to sing. I can still see George and John racing up to the stage with their mouths stuffed with hot dogs or whatever. The invitation to make our Cavern debut was given as soon as we finished A Thousand Stars *for them. They insisted we perform that very night. Everything happened completely spontaneously from that point.'*

On that Cavern debut in Nov '62, The

Chants, backed by the Beatles, performed a quartet of US R&B hits, Duke Of Earl, A Thousand Stars, 16 Candles and Come Go With Me before an enraptured audience. As Amoo again recalls:

'The Beatles themselves offered to back us when we told them we'd never worked with a band before. We then rehearsed four songs with them and then we ran home to tell all and sundry that we had "made it"! When Brian Epstein arrived at the Cavern that night he refused to allow the Beatles to back us, but they collectively persuaded him to change his mind — and when he heard us he invited us to appear on many subsequent appearances with them.'

Then there was the crucially-placed Derry Wilkie, the black lead singer of the otherwise white Derry & The Seniors, who were active between 1960 and 1962. They held a key to an important door for the Beatles, for they were the group that opened up the Hamburg scene to the Liverpool musicians, having been spotted playing at the 2i's Coffee Bar in London by Bruno Koschmider who ran the Kaiserkeller. They broke up after their Hamburg stint in 1960, but re-formed the following year, becoming the first Beat group from Liverpool to release an album, 1962's *Twist*

At The Top, although this was now credited to Wailin' Howie Casey & The Seniors, the group's founder and saxophonist elevated to the main billing despite the fact that Wilkie was still with them, now joined by a second vocalist, Freddy Fowell (later the comedian Freddie Starr). Wilkie would go on to join another local band, The Pressmen, with their only recording, Hallelujah, I Love Her So, included on the 1963 compilation *This Is Merseybeat*.

However, the most important black influence from their home city was arguably Harold Phillips, a Calypso rather than Beat or Rhythm & Blues performer — a Trinidadian who'd bestowed upon himself the faux-grandiose title Lord Woodbine — Woodbine referring to the brand of cigarettes he chain-smoked. During the fifties he started Liverpool's first steelpan orchestra and opened the New Colony Club in Toxteth. The Beatles (then the Silver Beatles) would play at his New Cabaret Artists Club on a few occasions in 1960, backing the strippers who performed there. He was certainly an early mentor to the Beatles.

Lord Woodbine accompanied the Beatles on their first trip to Hamburg with sometimes business partner Allan Williams, now immortalized as 'the man who gave the Beatles away'. The two appear in a prophetic photo, with four of Beatles (then a five-piece — John Lennon having remained in the van) pictured alongside Woodbine, Williams and his wife Beryl in front of the War memorial in Arnheim, Holland. It was August 1960 and they were travelling to Germany for their first stint in Hamburg — the memorial bearing the foretelling inscription 'Their Name Liveth For Evermore'.

Other notable figures on the local black music scene included Odie Taylor, Colin Areety, Steve Aldo, Sugar Deen and Vinnie Tow/Ismail. However, despite being in the right city, it was the wrong time for them — their skin colour very much holding them back in a less enlightened era.

The Beatles were the product of their environment, and coming into contact with people like Lord Woodbine would certainly have opened up new experiences for them to absorb, by way of both musical impressions and life lessons. They studied music by listening and watching — soaking in whatever appealed to them and building a wide repertoire, which they honed throughout long hours in Hamburg. Although Rhythm & Blues/Rock & Roll was the bedrock of their sound, there were other notable influences, not least country music, which was extremely popular in Liverpool, its sentimentality tugging at the city's Celtic heartstrings, whilst the music hall/variety Shows of previous generations provided a recurring theme. It should never be forgotten that Lennon & McCartney were natural tunesmiths, these weren't trained musicians — drinking in their influences from whatever stream of aural nourishment was at hand.

Having broken big in Britain via EMI's Parlophone imprint, and with Beatlemania in full-effect, the company's US affiliate, Capitol Records, shortsightedly declined to release the band's initial UK hits, holding out until they finally issued I Want To Hold Your Hand in the last week of 1963. The record would sit at the peak of the chart a little over a month later, the loveable mop tops who sang it sending shockwaves of joy throughout an unsuspecting America, still reeling in the aftermath of the JFK assassination.

Chicago-based R&B label, Vee-Jay, were the major beneficiaries of Capitol's poor judgement, taking a punt on these white boys from Liverpool by licensing their early recordings. This followed-on from the label enjoying an impressive run of hits with a white New Jersey group, The Four Seasons, who'd first find fame at Vee-Jay.

Vee-Jay issued two Beatles singles in the

US during 1963, but neither would make an impression. Philadelphia label Swan, who'd licensed She Loves You, saw their release suffer a similar fate. All of that changed when I Want To Hold Your Hand tumbled the walls, with Vee-Jay (and subsidiary label Tollie) hitting the jackpot as a consequence, placing four singles in the top three in '64, including a Number One for Love Me Do; their *Introducing The Beatles* album was only held off the top spot by Capitol's *Meet The Beatles*, which featured later material. Swan's reissue of She Loves You also topped the chart. It was a result of all these different labels vying for sales that that the Beatles found themselves historically monopolizing the top five positions on the US singles chart on April 4th '64.

A number of black artists would support the Beatles on their live tours. Mary Wells would be the first Motown act to appear in the UK as part of a Beatles bill, and The Chiffons would be one of the opening acts when they made their US debut in Washington (Feb 11th 1964). Further US tour dates would feature the likes of Brenda Holloway, The Ronettes, King Curtis and Bobby Hebb.

As the Beatles would cover black artists in their early years, many black artists would cover the Beatles — the appreciation was very much mutual. Black music references were there throughout their recording career, be it the self-depreciating title *Rubber Soul*, the Tamla Motown enthused Got To Get You Into My Life or the fact that their only record to credit another musician was Get Back, which featured keyboardist Billy Preston, who they'd first met when he was part of Little Richard's band earlier in the sixties.

Firm supporters of civil rights, they issued a press statement on their first US tour saying 'we will not appear unless Negroes are allowed to sit anywhere'. The Beatles refused to play in apartheid South Africa, and their music was banned from the airwaves in that country for a number of years following John Lennon's infamous 'more popular than Jesus' quote that caused such a rumpus in the same Southern States of the US where the black struggle was at its most stark. WAQY Birmingham, Alabama DJ Tommy Charles instigated a Beatles boycott that resulted in organized public bonfires of their records and merchandising, whilst hooded Ku Klux Klan members threatened to disrupt their concerts.

The Beatles would cease touring after the final US date at San Francisco's Candlestick Park (Aug 29th 1966), the bad vibes that followed the 'Jesus' quote taking its toll on the band, who would soon throw themselves into an unprecedented studio session that resulted in their *Sgt. Pepper* masterwork. Their subsequent album, *The Beatles*, would throw up its own dark legacy, due to its association with the notorious Manson murders.

Recorded and mixed in six hours at Abbey Road Studio 2 on June 11th 1968, Blackbird, like a number of tracks on the 'White Album' was believed to have been written whilst the four were on retreat in India with the Maharishi Mahesh Yogi, although Paul McCartney has since claimed to have written it in Scotland, where he'd bought a farmhouse. It consists of just three musical elements — the voice of its writer, his acoustic guitar pickings inspired, he said, by Bach's Bourrée In E Minor, and some blackbird warbling, sampled from the studio's effects library. The metronome type rhythm is courtesy of McCartney's tapping foot.

Although on the surface it's a beautiful song about overcoming adversity, which could apply to anyone, in the Barry Miles biography *Paul McCartney: Many Years From Now* (1997) the ex-Beatle explained:

'I had in mind a black woman, rather than a bird. Those were the days of the civil rights movement, which all of us cared passionately about, so this was really a song from me to a black woman, experiencing these problems in the States: "Let me encourage you to keep trying, to keep your faith, there is hope." As is often the case with my things, a veiling took place so, rather than say "Black woman living in Little Rock" and be very specific, she became a bird, became symbolic, so you could apply it to your particular problem.'

During a 2002 interview with DJ Chris Douridas on Dallas radio station KCRW, McCartney outlined this deeper, more specific meaning, telling the presenter that he wrote the track as a reaction to the building tensions in the black innercities of America, which had followed the assassination of Martin Luther King on April 4th 1968, just over a month after McCartney had returned from the band's Rishikesh retreat (McCartney spent time in Scotland that April, his trip North of the border endorsing his assertion that Blackbird was written there). During the KCRW interview he recalled:

'I was in Scotland playing on my guitar, and I remembered this whole idea of "you were only waiting for this moment to arise" was about, you know, the black people's struggle in the southern states, and I was using the symbolism of a blackbird. It's not really about a blackbird whose wings are

broken, you know, it's a bit more symbolic.'

During the same US tour, McCartney explained that 'bird' is British slang for girl, making 'blackbird' a synonym for 'black girl'. He elaborated in *Mojo* magazine in 2008:

'We were totally immersed in the whole saga which was unfolding. So I got the idea of using a blackbird as a symbol for a black person. It wasn't necessarily a black "bird", but it works that way, as much as then you called girls "birds"... "take these broken wings" was very much in my mind, but it wasn't exactly an ornithological ditty; it was purely symbolic.'

In his critical history of the Beatles, *Revolution in the Head*, first published in 1994, where he looks at each Beatles composition individually, Ian MacDonald highlighted the lyrics to Blackbird as 'a succinct metaphor for awakening on a deeper level', but failed to mention any civil rights associations. Having obtained details to be revealed in *Many Years From Now* prior to its publication, MacDonald added a note at the foot of the page in the 1997 update of his own book, dismissive of McCartney's recollections of his song's origins:

An alternative theory — with no support-

ing evidence — holds the song to be a metaphor for the black civil rights struggle in America (Manson adopted this line). In fact the formative mood of the song was gentle and romantic. McCartney sat on a windowsill and played it to the girl fans camped outside the house the first night his future wife Linda Eastman came over and stayed.

Why a gentle, romantic song can't be ambiguous, shielding a deeper meaning, I've no idea, but MacDonald and others had a point in questioning this disputed Beatles 'fact', revealed retrospectively, that had clear parallels with a viewpoint originated via Charles Manson's interpretation of the song's lyrics, which was that the Beatles were urging black people to rise up and revolt against the white establishment. Manson had, of course, attached significance to a number of tracks on the 'White Album', as discussed by prosecuting attorney Vincent Bugliosi in *Helter Skelter*, his best-selling account of the Manson orchestrated Tate-LaBianca murders and their sinister association with the LP. Manson believed America was on the verge of an impending apocalyptic race war, which he referred to as Helter Skelter, the title of another 'White Album' inclusion.

Having been accused of revisionism by

some, adapting the story to his own means in an effort to assign greater profundity to his lyrics, McCartney's account has now become part of Beatle mythos regardless of whether it can be proved or disproved. Ian MacDonald's words were slightly more conciliatory in the final edition of *Revolution in the Head*, published in 2005 after the KCRW interview. Dropping the 'no supporting evidence' line he now stated:

> For McCartney, Blackbird was a metaphor for the civil rights struggle in America, the subject being a black woman. Charles Manson made precisely this interpretation...

Piggies

K.J. DONNELLY

In his almost forensic analysis of the Beatles' recordings *Revolution in the Head*, Ian Macdonald calls Piggies '... an embarrassing blot on [George Harrison's] discography...' However, while the song certainly fails to rank among the Beatles' pantheon of greatest songs, it is in many ways distinctive and has a marked resonance to it. On the 'White Album', Piggies sits between Blackbird and Rocky Raccoon in a trio of animal-themed songs, a grouping that were considered among the most interesting on the album by Charles Manson. That Manson was attracted to the song is a point of interest, as is the song's musical arrangement, which was highly idiosyncratic. It is also a slightly troubling song, with its mock-classical affectation and children's rhyme-style, obscuring a sardonic and vindictive lyric that betrays a 'dark side' to the usually anodyne and user-friendly Beatles. Piggies seems to have a crude message about rich establishment figures which does not sit too well with the Beatles' prodigious wealth at this point. If Harrison and the other Beatles had not intended the song in any significantly political manner, then Charles Manson and his 'family' forcibly gave the song a more combative if not revolutionary association. Indeed, the first time I heard the song it was performed by a sound-alike rather than the Beatles and featured as incidental music in

Helter Skelter, the 1976 TV movie about the Manson family's murders and trial. It worked well in the film as a seemingly ironic counterpoint to the violent images, yet perhaps the contrast was in sound rather than lyrical content.

In the 'White Album', the Beatles managed to pull together a record that sold extremely well but mirrored the increasing fragmentation of the band, with each doing different solo songs and only a handful forged as a unit. This gave George Harrison an unprecedented space for his songs on the record. The visit to Rishikesh produced enough material for a double album but the individual group members found the time and energy for copious solo activities. Harrison experimented with prototype synthesizers and recording with Indian musicians. The first Apple album was Harrison's: his score for the Ur-psychedelic film *Wonderwall* (1968). His music for the film is a bold mixture of Indian classical music and psychedelic electronic rock jams. Lennon and Ono's *Unfinished Music no.1: Two Virgins* was also released on Apple Records a week after the 'White Album'. So the Beatles' album was bookended on their own record label by two effectively avant-garde albums by individual members of the group. In this context, the moments of experiment on the 'White Album' appear like a continuity although predominantly the double album has an accessible and arguably musically-conservative character.

According to Oded Heilbronner, in the early 1960s the 'ambivalent radicalism' of the Beatles led to controversy about their cultural and political orientation. This also came up as a subject of debate in cultural politics after the group broke up. Significantly, in May of 1968 when they began demoing the 'White Album' at Harrison's house Kinfauns, it was in the immediate wake of the Martin Luther King and Robert Kennedy assassinations. During May, Paris exploded into a near-revolution while the Prague Spring was crushed by Warsaw Pact tanks. It is striking how the time's potential for revolution is so little in evidence on the 'White Album'. There is no Street Fighting Man, merely the two Revolutions and perhaps a reference to the Cold War in Back In The U.S.S.R. As MacDonald suggests, they were espousing a 'Revolution in the Head' rather than an actual one. This is reminiscent of Antonio Gramsci's idea of a 'passive revolution', a slow and non-violent but nevertheless significant change. However, their approach was not met so charitably in some quarters. The editors at Chicago newssheet *Rising Up Angry* noted about the Beatles and the Rolling Stones, 'Unlike the Beatles and their passive resistance with All You Need is Love, and [Revolution], the Stones take a different look at things. They know you can't love a pig to death with flowers while he kicks the shit out of you.' Other things were on the Beatles' minds in 1968. At this point according to Denis O'Dell, who had been talking to United Artists about the third contracted Beatles film, the Fab Four were keen to film Tolkien's *Lord of the Rings*. Lennon was insistent upon playing Gandalf and he and McCartney had lunch with Stanley Kubrick, who dismissed the potential project. Should we be so dismissive of the Beatles' political attitude at the time? Piggies is a direct and crude comment on the establishment, and the chorus culminates in a startling call to violence that is utterly uncharacteristic in the Beatles output.

An earlier and clearly related Harrison song, Taxman from *Revolver* (1966), may have had a degree of anti-establishment sentiment to it but perhaps fits more clearly with a 'right wing libertarian' ideology (of the 'why should I pay taxes?' type). But Harrison had a right to complain. Songs he wrote that were published by the Northern Songs company saw more money going to shareholders Lennon and McCartney than to himself. Indeed, he wrote the bizarre and challenging private protest song Only A Northern Song precisely

to illustrate the point.

George Harrison had four of his songs on the 'White Album', which is the most of any Beatles album. Harrison's songs make up a subdivision of the Beatles' music. While the majority of songs are either McCartney's or Lennon's with a few collaborative efforts, Harrison's output was often marginalized and his songs were readily pushed aside by the band's principal songwriters. For example, while Harrison was 'allowed' a song on the iconic *Sgt. Pepper's Lonely Hearts Club Band* (1967), the droning Indian-inspired Blue Jay Way, other songs were rejected from here and the later *Magical Mystery Tour* (1967). For instance, It's All Too Much was recorded after the sessions for *Sgt. Pepper* but remained shelved and was not even considered for *Magical Mystery Tour*. Instead, It's All Too Much and Only A Northern Song were shunted onto the soundtrack for *Yellow Submarine* (1968). The Beatles were remarkably uninterested in this animated film project and did not even deign to supply their own voices for their cartoon screen characters. Underlining the quality of the song, It's All Too Much appears at the climax of the film and has a cathartic function exploiting its energy. It was in no way a substandard song and deserved more than being used as filler material for a film and soundtrack album in which the group had almost no interest. This is absolutely emblematic of Harrison's songs being overlooked or devalued by Lennon and McCartney.

Perhaps Piggies has been slightly overlooked, too. It is often the case with songs that we fail to notice the actual lyrical content because of its musical style (a good example is the Police's stalking song Every Breath You Take). Piggies mixes a mock-classical arrangement with the language of childhood and has something of the nursery rhyme or child's song about it. Indeed, if the lyrical content were less strident one can imagine it becoming a song beloved of children, rather like the earlier *Yellow Submarine*. A certain calculated naiveté was often evident in the late 1960s from the so-called 'flower children' and counterculture. At least partly, this originated in an assumption that children were honest, innocent and uncorrupted by 'straight' society (the establishment and conformity). With hindsight, this projection was more a metaphor for the youth culture's own idea about itself as pure and uncorrupted. But this does not tally with the snide worldliness and manipulative aspects of many involved with the counterculture. In Piggies, these two strains are awkwardly evident. The music and some of the words suggest a childish simplicity 'Have you see the little piggies...', which is brushed aside in an almost psychotic manner by the clear declaration about what the piggies might need. While children no doubt would misunderstand the song, an interesting aspect is that this 'childlike' approach allied with the accessible, bright major key music removes from the seriousness of the words in a startling misdirection.

After the song's opening verse which sets a scene with 'little piggies crawling in the dirt' (and the implication is that this dirt is in fact their own faeces), the second verse moves on to the 'bigger piggies', which clearly are human beings, 'in their starched white shirts.' These are not simply 'crawling' but 'stirring up the dirt'. While they doubtless are some incarnation of the establishment, this phrase suggests that the target might be journalists. The piggies 'always have clean shirts to play around in'. This is suggestive of the clean white shirts of 'white collar' workers (and perhaps even boring 'stuffed shirts') but also indicative of an erroneous sense of 'innocence' in their clean white apparel.

The next section of the song changes the chord structure: these piggies are rich and powerful, with significant support ('In their sties with all their backing, They don't care what goes on around'). They are indifferent to bad things that go on, which they might well be able to do something about, and quite possibly have actually caused. 'In their eyes there's something lacking'. These people are psychologically and emotionally stunted. 'What they need's a damn good whacking'. This is the real surprise. It is a direct call to violence. In fact, this marks the album's direct call for violent action along with the far more ambiguous Happiness Is A Warm Gun, as a counterpart to the seeming denial of revolutionary violence in *Revolution*, which stated (in more than a whisper) that you could count them out of it. The final verse describes these piggies as 'clutching forks and knives to eat their bacon'. While this may well simply be the wit of neat rhyming, the effect is strong: their 'bacon' is both their money and suggests that as pigs, they are cannibalistic in eating this meat (eating of themselves). The song finishes with a burst of pig grunting.

The particular sounds of the song are also one of its remarkable elements, and mark something of a counterpoint to the disgusted and aggressive tenor of the words. Ian Macdonald lists the musical resources that were used for the recording of Piggies. There was no drum kit, with Ringo Starr merely playing tambourine, accompanied by Harrison on acoustic guitar and McCartney on bass. The defining sounds were provided by assistant producer Chris Thomas on harpsichord and a nine-piece string ensemble (four violins, three violas, two cellos). Apart from helping with backing vocals, John Lennon added some sound effects of pigs grunting taken from an EMI sound effects recording.

The harpsichord is a baroque keyboard instrument that plucks strings. In principle, it is not too different from the guitar, with a plectrum-like quill sounding the metal strings once a key is depressed. Although the instrument was largely superseded by the piano, it did not fully disappear and came in for a small renaissance in the 1960s. The desire for new or at least distinctive sounds in recordings meant that marginal instruments could take the foreground. For instance, the harpsichord was used in Ron Goodwin's music for the Agatha Christie Miss Marple films starring Margaret Rutherford (*Murder She Said* [1961], *Murder at the Gallop* [1963], *Murder Most Foul* [1964]) and *Murder Ahoy!* [1964]). Heard today, the music perhaps sounds less baroque than 'sixties', an impression that is even stronger in Edwin Astley's harpsichord-featured music for television series *Randall and Hopkirk (Deceased)* (1969–70). This sound arguably makes Piggies less timeless than the rest of the album's songs.

Yet the song should sound less 'sixties', particularly due to its pseudo-classical sheen. More precisely, it uses a baroque sound characteristic of small ensemble art music from the seventeenth and eighteenth century as embodied by composers such as Monteverdi, Vivaldi, Handel and Johann Sebastian Bach. The song's performance parodies the stylized grace of courtly art music, with its busy harpsichord and emphasized and at times staccato string counter melodies. The melody of the song is simple and childlike, mostly on beat but with occasional basic syncopation. It is therefore very easy to sing and remains solidly in a Major key melody in A$\flat$ with simple alternation between tonic and dominant chords (I-V) for the opening of the verses. The next section of the song is marked out as different in a number of ways. The chords make an unorthodox change from B$\flat$m to C7 for 'in their sties with all their backing…' This interesting sound is compounded by a 'telephone voice' effect on the singing, filtering out high and low pitches. The culmination of 'what they need is a damn good whacking' is on bright primary chords (IV–V) moving upwards in pitch to the triumphant dominant on 'whacking' before returning to the tonic chord. This section has a more animated vocal performance, sung more open mouthed and with much vigour. Indeed, the song seems more joyous than comic.

Who is the target of this song? Harrison's music had contained a certain darkness before. Near the end of It's All Too Much, where Harrison appears to sing 'We are dead', it may be less one of the 'Beatles death clues' and more an oblique comment on the virtually moribund status of the group as a unity and their problematic inter-relationship. On some level with Piggies, Harrison might have been aiming his scatter gun of ire at the Beatles. Apple corporation had been set up to avoid paying tax and were simply throwing away money on vanity projects, most far more indulgent than Harrison's. While Harrison had earlier targeted tax collection in Taxman, Lennon and McCartney's publishing chicanery meant that they had also been taking his hard-earned money. Perhaps the little piggies are Harrison and Starr and the bigger piggies and McCartney and Lennon?

The more obvious target is the 'establishment' of which the Beatles were arguably becoming an important part. An additional verse which appeared in a later live Harrison recording, declared that the song's protagonists were 'down at the piggy banks, paying piggy thanks to the pig brother'. This seems to cement the object of the song as money and political bosses. The porcine metaphor was common at this point. While 'pig' became specific to police, at the time it was more generally applied to the establishment and the song makes an explicit engagement with counterculture attitudes to the rich and powerful.

As already noted, Piggies has an important position in the 'White Album's connection with the Manson Family. Charles Manson's interpretation of the 'White Album' as a Biblical communication alongside the Book of Revelation alights most clearly on a small number of songs: Helter Skelter (Manson's coming race war between black and white), Revolution 9 (the title of which plays directly upon the Bible's notorious apocalyptic Book of Revelation, chapter 9), Blackbird (about the side which will win the war) and Piggies (about the whites, and their rich white bosses). Indeed, at both Family massacres in August 1969 a reference to pigs had been left. After the murder at Sharon Tate's house, Susan Atkins had written 'Pig' on the front door and the next day, Patricia Krenwinkel had written 'Death to Pigs' on the wall in the blood of victims Leno and Rosemary LaBianca after sticking knives and forks into them. The song explicitly mentions forks and knives. Earlier, in July of 1969, Manson Family member and musician Bobby Beausoleil murdered Gary Hinman and wrote 'Political piggy' on a wall in his blood. This associational baggage adds a patina and frisson to the song. Violence is not metaphorical here. It is direct ('a damn good whacking'). But, like Maxwell's Silver Hammer on Abbey Road a year later, the seriousness of violence is misdirected by a childlike humour. Perhaps this humour provides a sonic metaphor at the song's conclusion. At the end of Piggies, following a moment of silence, there is an unusual coda of violent strong stabs accompanied by pig grunts. Just before this coda the music dramatically shifts key from Ab Major to minor. This is a reverse of the common procedure in baroque songs which liked to finish on a Major chord if in a minor key. In this case, it sounds a darker undercurrent at the conclusion of the song, and indeed suggests a more serious note for what initially appears to be a throwaway children's song.

Rocky Racoon

STEPHANIE FREMAUX

The Trial of Rocky Raccoon

15 August 1968

Opening statement by the presiding judge in the case of Dan v. Raccoon to members of the jury:

In the black mountain hills of Dakota in the year of our Lord 1890, the defendant Mr. Rocky Raccoon is accused of the attempted murder in the first degree, having entered the town's annual hoe down carrying a loaded, six-shooter pistol with the sole intent of shooting dead the plaintiff, Mr. Dan. The motivation for Mr. Raccoon's actions that night in question will be argued to be revenge for Dan's alleged wooing of saloon working girl Lil Magill, also known locally as Nancy, whom Rocky was said to have fancied.

The plaintiff argues that he drew his weapon first and shot acting in self-defence. The defendant has entered a plea of remorse and has since that fateful night begun preaching the good message on the local revival circuit.

Members of the jury, you will note Exhibit 4B — Gideon's Bible — taken by the defendant after the events of the evening in question. You will have the opportunity to examine this in greater detail as well as hear expert witness testimony from the attending doctor on call that night. Ladies and gentlemen of the jury, we are here to examine the facts and make a judgement on the value of one 'Rocky Raccoon.'

Rocky Raccoon, recorded on 15 August 1968, and *The Beatles*, released on 22 November 1968, hold a problematic, but arguably important, place within the Beatles' catalogue. The album was the first full-length release of new and original numbers since *Sgt. Pepper's Lonely Hearts Club Band* (1967), a concept album seen as a game changer both for the Beatles at the pinnacle of their career but also for the ways in which music could be recorded, packaged, and consumed as a complete artistic experience. The two LP disc set containing thirty songs held much promise in the wake of *Sgt. Pepper*. The 'White Album's legacy has been mythologized for its stories of band break-ups and make-ups, for the new ways in which the band were recording songs almost as solo artists in the studio as and when, rather than full-on collaborators laying down tracks in a matter of days, as well as heralding the arrival of John Lennon's new collaborator and soul mate, Yoko Ono. While the album holds a special intrigue with fans who speak of it fondly for its quirky uniqueness within the canon, critics and scholars are often dismissive, offering less than flattering comments of both the album and Rocky Raccoon towards what is often viewed as an anti-climax after *Sgt. Pepper*'s acclaim.

Of the album, *New Musical Express* (*NME*) critic Alan Smith writing in November 1968 noted that the tracks did not 'possess the overall pattern of a *Sgt. Pepper*, and neither do most of them have the compelling unreality of that uniquely special journey into the mind.' *Melody Maker* journalist Alan Walsh argued, 'I doubt this album will stand as high in the world's opinion as *Sgt. Pepper* did'. With the passage of time, some argue that perhaps we have just grown to take the Beatles for granted: 'we hear the Beatles so often involuntarily that it's easy to forget to listen to them deliberately. If you can hear past the tensions involved [...] it is a glorious, giddy, liberating hoot [...]'.

While it might be easy to understand the 'White Album's failings when compared to *Sgt. Pepper*, Rocky Raccoon does not fair much better in the scholars' estimation. Of the song, respected Beatles scholar Ian MacDonald describes it as a 'jokey ad-lib,' and a 'faintly amusing squib' that 'seems to be leading somewhere until its glib closing lines.' Musicologist Walter Everett only considers it in his detailed analysis of the Beatles' output because he is aware it is a fan favourite but otherwise, he finds 'nothing else particularly noteworthy in the song's musical or poetic content.' Arguably, however, when Rocky Raccoon is placed in context it becomes an important signifier in Paul McCartney's songwriting development, foreshadowing the themes and characters that would dominate his solo career output.

McCartney's earliest solo compositions as a Beatle are rich in themes of nostalgia and utilize characters that come to represent slice of life stories captured in the middle and often with no conclusion or resolution. These include Drive My Car (1965) and Penny Lane (1967) to Your Mother Should Know (1967), Ob-La-Di, Ob-La-Da, Martha My Dear and Rocky Raccoon (all 1968). During McCartney's solo career and with his post-Beatles band, Wings, these character-focused stories would come to be focal points on his albums. These include Teddy Boy (1970), Uncle Albert/Admiral Halsey (1971), McCartney's first US number one single, Another Day (1971), Mrs. Vandebilt (1974), Magneto And Titanium Man (1975), Temporary Secretary (1980), Jenny Wren (2005), Mr. Bellamy (2007), and On My Way To Work (2013).

When considering McCartney's trajectory as a solo songwriter, one does wonder if because of the high standards and early unprecedented success of the Lennon-McCartney songwriting team, McCartney became unfairly held to higher standards and expectations as a solo composer. Both MacDonald and Everett's analyses frequently point to instances in McCartney's songbook when the Beatle was perhaps singing out of tune, or delivering uncomplicated and unchallenging work. Even McCartney's early solo career was heavily criticized by the music press at the time. However, Womack's (2010) study of the Beatles and the role of autobiography is useful to draw upon in considering the value of songs like Rocky Raccoon. Womack argues that the Beatles' focus on working in the studio from 1965 onwards helped to foster 'an increasing interest in storytelling and rudimentary ethical philosophy.' In the case of Rocky Raccoon's cinematic narrative in the Western genre, McCartney's seemingly jokey tale opening with an accentuated

comical accent setting the scene lends itself to be read as a cautionary tale of what can happen when hope and rationality are abandoned for hot-headed revenge and one-upmanship. Fortunately, Rocky gets another chance after his botched showdown with Dan, heeding the lessons from the saloon bedroom copy of Gideon's Bible he initially rejects.

Even though McCartney is not making any strong religious message, the story of Rocky's trials and new found faith are in keeping with the themes and motifs found in Americana, frontiers literature and early twentieth century Westerns. In this way, Rocky Raccoon also signifies McCartney's voracious appetite for new cultural influences. The late 1960s saw a resurgence in the popularity of the singer/songwriter troubadour with Bob Dylan's western tinged *John Wesley Harding* (1967) and the rise of the Western genre in cinema. Both Miles (1998) and McCartney in more recent interviews and work have argued that while Lennon might have had the counterculture look and anti-establishment, 'angry young man' attitude, it was McCartney who was most interested in the avant-garde and underground scene: from vaudeville, home cinema, and photography, to underground art and literature, McCartney had the commercial sensibilities and business acumen to understand how to balance those varied interests for a mainstream audience through universal themes like nostalgia for the 'good ol' days' amongst a time of increasing racial tensions, social unrest, and the brink of war in Vietnam.

The Beatles retreat to Northern India under the spiritual tutelage of Maharishi Mahesh Yogi in February 1968 allowed McCartney to play and create with other musicians including Donovan and the Beach Boys' Mike Love. Both McCartney and Lennon ended up writing a large number of songs on the trip, many of which ended up on the 'White Album'. For McCartney as a songwriter it can be seen as a period of exploration with different approaches and styles. Speaking about the output from the India trip, he notes how he would write songs as if they were poems to be remembered, revised, and worked on later in the studio. With Rocky Raccoon McCartney liked the quirkiness of it: 'it's me writing a play, a little one-act play giving [the characters] most of the dialogue.' And though it can be argued that the Beatles had begun to be solo composers well before the 'White Album', late 1967/68 was a key turning point — one of directionless after the death of their long dedicated and doting manager Brian Epstein. Despite the Beatles' increasing autonomy in their crea-

tive decision-making, Epstein still had influence over them and good judgement. Without Epstein, the Beatles rushed into making an experimental TV film *Magical Mystery Tour* and disregarded producer George Martin's advice to pare down *The Beatles* into a tighter, more coherent one-disc LP. Maybe it was only George Harrison who went to India seriously open to the possibilities of spiritual enlightenment, while the others saw it as a bit of a lark and a chance to get away from England, the media, fans, and fame. But through McCartney's songwriting output and processes during this time, it arguably became a chance for him to reflect on his craft and how to develop his output around specific themes and styles.

In closing, perhaps McCartney's insight into the genesis of Rocky Raccoon is the key to how the 'White Album' with all of its seemingly mismatched songs, snatches of songs, and sound collage should be approached by the listener — as a kind of play or variety show. Womack sees the album as a 'song cycle' where the 'countrified' style of Rocky Raccoon segues naturally 'from the disquieting universe of cowboys, gunplay, and saloons into a gentle paean about nostalgia and loss' with Ringo Starr's Don't Pass Me By, from saloon hoedown to beer hall choruses. And like the Western film frontier mythology centred around the wilderness (the individual, self-knowledge, self-interest), nature (purity, experience, savagery), and the idea of The West (the frontier, tradition, the past), these themes are firmly embedded throughout the songs included on the 'White Album' and Rocky Raccoon embodies each of these mythologies as well as a lifetime of McCartney-esque themes and situations in its three and a half minutes. So while some may feel the song has a 'flimsy premise' with

a guitar part that 'gets old quickly', Rocky Raccoon like the rest of the 'White Album' should be valued for what it is — the Beatles not taking themselves too seriously and creating music while having the time of their lives before the cracks in the veneer of 'The Beatles' became visible to all.

Madam foreman, in the case of Dan v. Rocky Raccoon have the members of the jury reached a verdict?

Don't Pass Me By

Sonic Youth's STEVE SHELLEY interviewed by STEVE SHEPHERD

STEVE SHEPHERD (SSH): The big question is that Sonic Youth did the *The Whitey Album*...

STEVE SHELLEY (SS): You know that when I joined the band, on the schedule was to do the 'White Album'. Thurston [Moore] said: 'we're going to record the "White Album"' and I'm like: 'it's my favourite album of all time'! That was an amazing thing to hear, although it never happened!

One idea about the concept that I really

liked was that we were going to farm out a few tunes. The tunes that stylistically didn't match us we were going to give to other groups. Saccharine Trust were in a West Coast jazz phase at the time and we said: 'let's give them Savoy Truffle'... ideas like that... I loved the idea... I was very excited about it.

SSH: Why didn't it happen?

SS: We just lost our steam on the idea... Pussy Galore did the *Exile on Main St.* album and we thought — we don't have to do that now!

SSH: Were the Beatles one of the groups that you felt were a touchstone?

SS: Lee [Renaldo] and I were enormous fans but they were not a group that came up in rehearsals. Then it was more The Stooges and Neu! Can, Neil Young, The Velvets. They were kept a bit in the distance but they were already in my DNA.

SSH: Is the 'White Album' still your favourite album?

SS: I think so, because of the diversity of it; because even thirty or forty years after first hearing it there are so many different things on it. I think it's one of John's best periods: Julia, Glass Onion... all the John material is really striking for that period. To go from Good Night to Revolution 9... So the diversity, and where they were as a band. There's a melancholy feel over the album, even the joyful songs. They brought in the guitar fingerpicking from India that was not there before — apart from maybe Yesterday. Dear Prudence is one of my favourite songs of all time. People get distracted by some of the tunes they don't like as much, which has never bothered me!

SSH: I agree with you about John's writing, it's a culmination of all the strands of the Beatles coming together. There are certain sounds, vocal ticks that they may repeat, but they never do it as well as on the 'White Album'. It's very hard to define because of the diversity of sound. Everybody gets a voice.

It's a bit of a stretch, but maybe that is because it's a 'white album', the planeness of the sleeve doesn't distract you from the music. It's about songwriting. Not 'back to basics' but it's just about the music that's on there.

SS: One thing I really like about the album too is the little incidental sounds bits and segues and connections... the fragment of songs that didn't make it. The classical guitar being played... I assumed it was George and then I found it was from a library album! That all kept me going for years...

SSH: I think Ringo's drumming is the best he ever did. Because of the diversity of sound on the record, you realize what a sympathetic player he was... he's feeling the music, it's very subtle but you notice him without being too pushy. I like Don't Pass Me By. He once said that he only knew three chords on the guitar and three chords on the piano. He wrote it at No.10 Admiral Grove. What do you think of it?

SS: I like it a lot. I'm attracted to the recording, the cacophony that surrounds it, the violin coming and going, the drums playing in a not-exactly delicate manner. I've always been attracted to the 'royal mess' that it is!

SSH: What about Ringo as a drummer?

SS: I think he's amazing. He's the fourth element in so many of those songs. I believe that if he hadn't been there they would not have been as good as they were. He contributes in a way that is not always easily measured. When you have such a great group, what everybody gives to it is so important.

It's not a drumming thing, it's a songwriting thing. I don't think of his 'fills' or how fancy he can get. It's more about doing the right thing for the right tune, what his part in the chemistry is. He was there for some of the greatest songwriting and recordings from that era.

SSH: What about his technique as a drummer?

SS: He's perfect. I know that when he joined he was the more experienced musician. Around the 'White Album' we got to hear

the most interesting parts of his playing. I like that the Beatles knew when *not* to have drums. That makes him even better when he is there. I always appreciated groups where it was possible for someone to sit it out.

SSH: I read somewhere that the drums on Don't Pass Me By were put though a Leslie organ cabinet speaker. How difficult as a drummer is it to get it right? Is it immediately obvious? How would Ringo know what was 'right'?

SS: I guess sometimes it's extremely obvious. When you have a song that is as delicate as Julia you know that no one needed to add to that. That's the easiest kind of decision. But it's like architecture: does the song need a skeleton from the drummer and if so, then what is the skeleton doing? How is the drum part keeping the song together or strengthening it? Is it heavy work, or light work? All those questions come in to the game. Sometimes that's the most gratifying part of songwriting, making those decisions. A lot of it is shooting in the dark. You are just searching, which can also be fun. Sometimes things just fall into your lap at times and it feels magical.

SSH: It's funny that for the first ten or fifteen years or so, you have your favourite 'White

Album' track and then suddenly it changes and you start digging Why Don't We Do It in the Road?

SS: Yeah, like Long Long Long. I probably didn't pay attention to that when I was a younger person but as time went on the attack of that song became one of my favourites. It became such a special song.

SSH: Do you think Paul ever had a drummer that was so *simpatico*?

SS: That's the word. I don't think it matters if a drummer is technically better: it's about the time that they spent together. These shared interests and shared experiences that make it special. That's why it's so hard to answer the question about how good Ringo is: I don't really care. He's the one that was there for the experiences that only they had and it comes out in these records that we still listen to. It's also not just that someone was there but you had to know enough to be an 'antennae' for what was happening. You had to react and respond and move with the times. Ringo used what he had for those years.

SSH: He's a very emotionally intelligent drummer.

SS: Yes, he had the tools. He had to work in that situation.

SSH: He always gets it right. Most drummers in the 1960s were playing a basic 4/4 beat. You know Ringo is always on the money. The 'White Album' is a really good ensemble record. I think they were disappointed with *Sgt. Pepper*; it was not what they thought it would be. They weren't trying to better *Sgt. Pepper* but they were trying to make the record that they wanted to make in terms of diversity and range and songwriting and they came pretty close. How many copies do you have?

SS: I have four or five.

SSH: Was the 'White Album' your favourite Beatles record instantly?

SS: I think it was a favourite very early on. We used to put our favourite LPs on a cassette and I remember it being on a C90 so that we could listen to it in the car!

SSH: When you were making *Daydream Nation* were you thinking of the 'White Album'? Were you conscious it was a 'statement', opening up possibilities?

SS: No. When you are in the middle of making a record it's probably best not to think like that. When we were in that place it's more that you are in the middle of the work. We were on a cycle of record/tour, which we later did break to do something different.

SSH: The 'White Album' is the album where the Beatles gave the most, and gave the most as a group. It's the band being 'grown up'. They can still remember who they are but they are also being changed by being 'the Beatles'.

But they are not being too damaged by the process yet so that they can't stand each other. There is just enough to make this one great statement. It's very 'hermetic'?

SS: The 'White Album' makes its own universe. When you listen to it you are in 'White Album' world. As a teenager, you are alone or in a strange place and if you put the 'White Album' on you are in a world that you can immediately relate to.

Why don't we do it in the road?

JAX GRIFFIN

When I set out to do a photographic portrayal of the song Why Don't We Do It In the Road I wanted to look past just the song's sexual connotations, without disregarding them. I also wanted to speak to a modern audience while staying true to themes the Beatles represented. The most obvious of these themes pertaining to this song in particular is the idea of 'free love'. Perhaps no other band more embodies the 'sex, love, and rock and roll' attitude of the 1960s than the Beatles and they not only sang about it but made their voices heard

on the social stage as well, both during their time as a group and after their break-up.

This is what ultimately led me to the idea of dealing with protest in some way — a right that has long been part of society but has become an especially hot subject in recent times. I really wanted to represent and sort of 'mash-up' protest culture so that the image isn't representative of one particular group and I'm ultimately happy with the outcome of that endeavour.

Fig.4 © Jax Griffin

I Will

MARK GOODALL

'Romanticism is emotion rather than reason; the heart opposed to the head'

George Sand

Paul McCartney's music is largely defined by an engagement with the romantic tradition. Granted, he is famous for strident Beatles rockers such as I Saw Her Standing There, She's A Woman and, on the 'White Album', Back in The U.S.S.R. and Helter Skelter and the odd exploration into the realm of the avant-garde. And yet it is his skill at combining beautiful melodic and harmonic elements expressed through a warm and lyrical singing voice that down the ages has captured audiences. I personally find the representation of Lennon as an 'authentic' rebel figure and McCartney as a composer of 'granny music' tiresome and clichéd. Aside from the inaccuracy of this surface characterization within the Beatles' *oeuvre* and beyond (together with the equally crass representation of groups like the Rolling Stones and The Animals as somehow more 'real' than the Beatles), it seems preposter-

ous to claim that fake Americana, the grandiose statement and the overblown protest song are somehow more important than the tune that lifts the spirits by expressing passionate, emotional feelings of love.

It has been argued that I Will 'anticipates the relaxed sentimentality' of McCartney's blossoming solo work. Certainly the sonic properties of the song are echoed on McCartney's first solo LP. Aside from the soft and pleasant sound of the track, accentuated by McCartney's mellifluous voice, the sung rather than played bass part and the warm Martin acoustic guitar picking, it is worth considering how this song, and the Beatles romantic tradition in general, connects with wider thinking on the psychology of romantic love...

The capacity for human love is as timeless as the development of humankind and yet remains a mysterious phenomenon. It's no surprise that music, another mystical singularity, has tried to capture and express the many dimensions of romantic love. This has occurred through poetry, prose and modern art forms such as film. However, it is arguably through music, where words and sounds are combined most effectively, that the emotional elements of romantic love work best. As a 'young' art form popular music and rock'n'roll seems ideally placed to represent the first romantic feelings of love as experienced by young people (principally teenagers). Romantic love in the epoch of the Beatles developed into a phase of 'entitlement, individualism and narcissism' and songs became less about the nature of romance and more fixated on hedonistic sexual relationships and the tragedy of doomed and illicit teenage romance ('rock music has always basically been erotic'); the famous equation rock+roll=sex. The medieval concept of 'courtly love', while attractive, dissolved with the gradual development of rock and a concurrent more cynical attitude to relationships. At this time an arguably more realistic (whilst at the same time pornographic) portrayal of love emerges with a wilder and apparently freer conception of emotions connected to love and sex. Carl Jung, one of the Beatle heroes who appeared on the cover for *Sgt Pepper's Lonely Hears Club Band*, had tried to extend this understanding of romance to incorporate non-Western (especially Eastern) aspects of the understanding of love and the idea that there could be a collective experience of love that resulted in a path to universal consciousness.

If 'Romantic love is the recognition and affirmation of both the self and someone else' then I Will perfectly captures that mode. As the above George Sand epigraph suggests, romantic expression of the kind found in McCartney's *oeuvre* derives from a straight attempt, without intellect, at hitting emotional nerves and evoking through sound the state of romantic love. There is here an obvious connection with the lyric poet tradition of Goethe, Wordsworth and Christina Rossetti and modern poets such as Auden etc. (albeit a simplified version of this). McCartney's tendency toward the pastoral (also found on Mother Nature's Son) links to the romantic tradition in classical art, music and poetry, where an emphasis on the natural world, imagination and emotion as the true source of pleasure, as opposed to the artificiality of the city and the rationality of science, was key. McCartney was to follow this in his own personal life, moving to a remote area of Scotland and taking up vegetarianism (and thus was arguably more ecologically minded than the supposedly deeper, spiritual George Harrison). Sentimentality, another dimension to the romantic ideal is also evident in I Will but in terms of human experience is as true an expression as violence, hate or depression.

It is perhaps the idea of rock as something dangerous that critics compare unfavourably with the McCartney lyric ballad style. But anyone sensitive to the direct experience music can offer, in contrast to the slight distance one gets from the written word, can feel what romantic love is like through an effective composition. Songs, with their dynamics, sound artistry and use of the human voice (especially notable in modern popular music where sound is recorded very faithfully), capture the sometimes difficult set of emotions connected to love and desire. The lyric, with its highly individual voice, is the main achievement of the Romantic movement, and I Will acts as a late expression of this tendency through the art of the popular song.

Robert A. Johnson has argued that 'roman-tic love is the single greatest energy system in the Western psyche… it has supplanted religion as the arena in which men and women seek meaning, transcendence, wholeness and ecstasy'. Love cannot re reduced to scientific formulae and attempts to do so have failed miserably. Clearly, the Beatles, with their many songs about being 'in love', made a powerful contribution to this energy system. I Will pays homage to the earlier Beatles love songs (albeit rendered in a more folk pastoral style than the doo-wop arrangements of a song like Yes It Is for example) and was a brief but elegant contribution, at the twilight of their career as a group, and as the drugs and violence and disaffection began to take hold, to this mystical dimension. What is expressed in the song is a myth, but it is a beautiful one.

Julia

JEREMY DYSON

A reminiscence

I was late to the 'White Album' though early to the Beatles.

Their songs had found their way inside me by the time I was nine. Growing up in the 1970s they were still recent history — though they were already as culturally monolithic then as now. My father was a member of a postal record library and LPs would arrive monthly in a heavy cardboard slipcase — wrapped in brown paper — which would be listened to, recorded to cassette and dutifully shipped back. Although the primary borrowings were classical my mother would slip some of her Radio 2-ish pop choices into the order. Glen Campbell's *Greatest Hits*, *The Sound of Bread*, *The Hollies 20 Golden Greats*. One month it was the Beatles 'Red' and 'Blue' albums. She was a rock and roller — a fifties teen with a passion for Buddy Holly. Already a mother by the time Beatlemania struck she wasn't a fanatic herself. But she liked the songs — probably unaware that the group took their name from her teen idol's backing band.

I would put on these pop albums myself. I liked a good tune and was immediately caught, particularly by the blue album which had more going on, even to my untutored virgin ears. The sound effects and atmosphere and occasional mystery and melancholy. I already knew I preferred songs in a minor key — having worked out the difference aged five — via Andy Williams Can't Get Used To Losing You. I liked that it sounded sadder then the other songs around it when it came on the cassette in the car.

Having caught the Beatles bug, I asked dad

if I could get more Beatles on the next order. *Rubber Soul* and then *Revolver* followed — and after that *Magical Mystery Tour* and the *Hey Jude* compilation. That was the extent of my collection and would remain so for another twenty years, even though I started buying my own records aged twelve — fuelling a growing addiction by performing magic shows at children's parties. Why no Beatles purchases throughout my teen years and early twenties? Because punk had struck just prior to my coming of age — and I was firmly on that side of the divide — 'no Elvis, Beatles, or Rolling Stones' was a rule I understood instinctively. Nothing could have been less cool — I already had the hipster urge.

Turn the LP over — fast forward twenty years — and by the mid-nineties those restrictions had begun to lift. Thanks first to proto grunge — loud/quiet bands such as Pixies, Hüsker Du, and Nirvana — and then to Brit-pop bands — not just Oasis, but less chart-bound acts like Teenage Fanclub, Dodgy — referencing the Beatles became hip again. It really did take that long though. Earlier Beatles nods felt gauche, lacking in taste and style — E.L.O. or Tears for Fears. McCartney and Harrison solo output didn't help — at least not with younger music fans.

So — I started buying the Beatles albums on vinyl — owning them for the first time, which I find astonishing now, given that I'd been amassing a record collection for fifteen years. I began with the ones I'd had and loved and then, tentatively I moved out to the ones I hadn't, the ones I'd never heard even. Yes — a music lover who had never listened to at least half the Beatles output.

Let It Be was one of those albums, along with *Abbey Road* and the 'White Album'. I was most suspicious of that trio because the band sported beards and moustaches by then, at least in my mind's eye, and I'd always resisted the beards and the moustaches.

It was the studio experimentation I loved, the wild unbridled play and creativity. What came after was associated with dryer and more earnest pretention — at least in my imagination. I think this was because of the kids at school who I knew liked that phase, and later the ones at Jewish youth clubs — the acoustic-guitar strumming, soft-rock loving, cripplingly uncool and hatefully self-confident fools who would sit in the middle of a circle and lead everyone in a round of *Let It Be*. I didn't like the 'Mother Mary' in Let It Be either. So Christian — right on the edge of happy clappy Godspell-rock — the least cool thing in the world. Ugh.

So, the 'White Album' arrived late in my consciousness — along with *Dark Side of the Moon*, Neil Young, Steely Dan and all the other stuff labelled verboten hippy shit in my teenage years. My adult self, it seemed, was able to detect flickers of creative interest there worth investigating.

In fact, as I remember, it was first absorbed properly during a bout of flu — driving back alone from London to Leeds in my shuddering little Mini, chugging up the M1, shivering and yearning for my bed (I'd already transferred it to cassette from LP for listening to in the car)

Some tracks I took to immediately — the ones that sounded most like my beloved studio period Beatles — Glass Onion, Dear Prudence, Back In The U.S.S.R. Some I was deeply dubious about — one notch above novelty filler — Piggies, Rocky Raccoon. Some were a racket — Why Don't We Do It In The Road. Some were 'interesting' — Helter Skelter, Happiness Is A Warm Gun. One jumped out as unequivocally beautiful and a development from the Beatles I knew of old. And that would be Julia.

It was Lennon's of course — and it was only then — aged twenty-eight — was I able to fully distinguish between their voices in a group context — despite having grown up fully cognisant of their solo work. I say of course, because as I grew into something approximating adulthood it was Lennon's voice that started to speak to me most directly. And when I say voice I mean that in the 'writerly' way. I could sense he was a truth teller — very different from McCartney who was hard to shake from his naïve 'thumbs aloft' (as they used to say in the *NME*) naïvely optimistic eighties persona. Harrison I'd always been suspicious of because of the overt religion (which bothers me much less now — but that's getting older for you). Lennon seemed much closer in spirit to Lydon — still the ultimate attitudinal benchmark in many ways then.

But with Lennon you also got the beauty. The plaintive, heart-holding melancholy gorgeousness of his melodies, and their delicate execution. The liquid tune that made you want to listen to it again as soon as you'd got to the end. But it wasn't stultifyingly perfect. There was something unformed about it, unfinished — the antitheses of the finalised and definitive statements of Strawberry Fields Forever and I Am The Walrus. They were concrete statements — slabs of Art. This was pure emotion.

That first time — or first few times listening to it — I assumed it was a love song. 'Half of what I say is meaningless' — Julia perhaps standing for Yoko. I was ignorant of Lennon's family history and the tragedy of his mother so I heard it differently to how I hear it now — perhaps with a layer of romance — that bares no relation to the agonising truth the song is actually communicating.

And yet beneath whatever I thought it was about I sensed the authentic yearning, and the impossible sadness — assuming it the apotheosis of the melancholic minor key that I'd always loved in the Beatles (and not exclusive to Lennon), starting with Michelle, working forward to Yesterday, then Eleanor Rigby. The sad songs were the best. What I was hearing here — without realizing it initially was Lennon feeling his way from popsongs and through art songs into something very different, something completely new — confessional truth, deep, deep pain rendered as unadorned beauty. It was the precursor to the *Plastic Ono Band* LP and it is still a rare form.

Maybe this is one of the things that thrills most about the Beatles — they didn't just do one thing first — they did many things first. This song may well be the purest use of deep pain in all of popular music — an alchemical transformation of wound into beauty. Unembellished save for one piece of delicate magic: the double tracking of Lennon's voice as he calls his dead mother's name — resulting in a kind of subtle chorusing that turns his vocal into something ghostly. I remember hearing an interview with producer Mike Chapman talking about the rare quality that Debbie Harry's voice had when it was tracked with itself. The iterations combined somehow reacted with each other and something magical happened. Lennon's voice has the same quality. George Martin said John always hated hearing it as it was and was forever asking for slap-back echoes and ADT to disguise it from himself. And yet here the effect is not to disguise but to amplify the personal — aptly redolent of someone haunted by their own ghost — or the ghost of the child they once were.

If I were to chuck all the other songs away of the thirty on the album and was only allowed to keep one it would without question be this. The specific pain it recounts is Lennon's own and yet the universal it touches is everyone's. A few years ago, I met a wise French oncologist at dinner when we were on holiday in Cornwall. I can't remember how we got there but after a relatively short conversation — certainly no longer than the span between a main course to coffee — he said 'You know — I never know whether life is a happy sadness or a sad happiness'. Immediately I understood exactly what he meant. I'd felt it all my life — probably since first noticing the draw of a minor key courtesy of Andy Williams — and the perfect soundtrack to the sentiment is Julia. The personal loss was Lennon's and he made it articulate everybody else's in the simplest most beautiful way imaginable. The sound of life itself, in a three-minute pop song.

Birthday

CORY STRAND

I remember the first time I heard John Lennon's How Do You Sleep? It was a weekend afternoon in 1996, and I was an angry fifteen-year-old kid who listened to very little music beyond Slayer, Deicide, Napalm Death, the Melvins, and Mudhoney. The speed and anti-authoritarian vitriol that defined thrash and death metal, along with the oppressive and emotive sludge of grunge, were the sorts of sounds and attitudes I gravitated towards; the focused aggression and murky audio impenetrability of the music itself helped to define what little sense of self I had back then (I was still a few years away from my discovery of Japanese noise and psychedelia, which would crack my mind wide open to music's outer reaches.)

My father, a rock drummer and a lifelong Beatles fanatic who grew up during the sixties and seventies, burst into my room and handed me Lennon's *Imagine* CD, telling me that I had to hear How Do You Sleep? (He also mentioned that How Do You Sleep? was the only good song on the record, the rest of which he described as 'overrated'.) My father believed How Do You Sleep? was one of the angriest songs ever written, and that its pervasive sense of simmering rage and bitterness would appeal to me. He explained that Lennon had written the song as a pointed attack on Paul McCartney, whom Lennon retroactively viewed as having betrayed the 'White Album'-era Beatles' tendency toward experimentation, iconoclasm, and musical radicalism. Post-Beatles McCartney had become an establishment square, and it pissed Lennon off.

Since that afternoon in 1996, How Do You Sleep? has never left my mind. Whenever I listen to the 'White Album, especially some of the more complex, heavy, and primal songs like Helter Skelter, Yer Blues and Happiness Is A Warm Gun I find myself thinking of the growing aesthetic rift between Lennon and McCartney, a rift that gave way to an embittered animus between the two for years after the dissolution of the Beatles. The direction each writer would ultimately take in their post-Beatles solo careers was previewed by their songwriting contributions to the 'White Album': it isn't difficult to see that McCartney's work was becoming more regressively minimal, as simple rock and roll compositions like Back In The U.S.S.R. and pop-tinged charmers like Ob-La-Di, Ob-La-Da indicate, and that Lennon's work, evidenced by cuts like Revolution 9 and Everybody's Got Something To Hide Except Me And My Monkey (my father's favourite song on the 'White Album'), was heading toward a much more open and progressively experimental plateau. That aesthetic divide is part of what makes the 'White Album' such a timeless piece of work for me: it's a constant intellectual and artistic battle between two visionaries to simultaneously define and shatter the notion of what a Beatles album should be. Its songs reek of buried angers and personal frustrations.

Perhaps no song better captures that buried anger and frustration than the seemingly innocuous Birthday. McCartney wrote Birthday in a single day, banging it out on a piano at Abbey Road studios. McCartney wanted the song to have more of a 'contemporary' rock and roll feel, so it morphed into its more guitar-heavy form when the band laid it down for the album. In a certain sense, perhaps owing to its simple and somewhat spontaneous composition, the song *feels* like a toss-off: there isn't much to it aside from its bright guitar riffs, chanted vocals, and bombastic drums. It opens side three of the record and two minutes later it's over, giving way to some of the Beatles' heaviest and most oppressive cuts. It isn't a toss-off, though — Birthday is a door, a gateway that draws the listener in and drags them deep into the Beatles at their most primal, ferocious, unrelenting, and caustic. The song's outwardly cheery disposition is a guise, a bandage over the weeping psychic wound that was Lennon and McCartney's disintegrating personal and professional partnership, an account of competitive bitterness and resentment that defined both writers' relationship to one another and to the Beatles as a now-fractured artistic entity. Birthday is both pop *par excellence*, a song stripped down to its most basic and necessary elements and unadorned by the group's typical lyrical obscurantism, and a scathing blast of guitar-driven proto-metal that showcased the Beatles' engagement with the heavier side of rock music circa 1968.

The late sixties of England and the United States saw an explosion of heavier, guitar-centric recordings by bands that ushered in a new era of loud, minimalistic rock devastation. It was a return to rock's Satanic roots via the simplicity of Robert Johnson, but drowned under tidal waves of guitar distortion and excess. The Jimi Hendrix Experience, Blue Cheer, The Yardbirds, Cream, the Who, and Jethro Tull had all released multiple recordings by 1968 that pushed both the sheer physicality of volume and an anti-authoritarian ideology to the forefront of their work; there was an unconscious and shared desire between these groups, it seemed, to both rediscover rock and roll's missing sense of danger and rebellion and to reposition the genre as a fertile breeding ground for audial experimentation and aesthetic radicalism. Jimi Hendrix's work with guitar/amplifier feedback and Pete Townshend's work with pure live volume during the period illustrate this desire; the Beatles were aware enough of this evolution for McCartney to maintain that Helter Skelter was written in an attempt to make a Beatles recording that was even louder and more damaged than The Who's

I Can See For My Miles (I'd say the Beatles succeeded there). The Velvet Underground's 1968 opus *White Light/White Heat*, with its sidelong mesmerizer Sister Ray, took Hendrix's feedback experimentation and Townshend's volume fetishization and turned it into flat-out feedback *worship,* a summoning up and channeling out of all sorts of feelings of disenchantment and cultural resentment, blasted through screaming amplifiers and fuzz pedals. In the far eastern reaches of Japan, where the Beatles had toured just a few years earlier in 1966, an even more damaged form of feedback-drenched anti-establishment rock was rearing its head in the form of Les Rallizes Denudes, a group whose artistic mission, according to Julian Cope, was a 'total sensory assault of the culture' that would make the Velvets look like the Byrds in comparison. All of this was heavy art damage for the sake of itself. It's hard for me to imagine that the Beatles weren't aware of, and were taking in and synthesizing, at least some of this stuff and bringing its influence to bear on their own music; after all, Lennon's work with partner Yoko Ono on the 1969 album *Unfinished Music no. 2: Life with the Lions* offers up what is to me one of the most intense onslaughts of guitar noise ever committed to tape, not to mention their other avant-garde musical experiments together (the albums *Two Virgins* and *Wedding Music*).

All four members of the Beatles travelled to India in 1968 to study Transcendental Meditation with the Maharishi Mahesh Yogi. Much of the 'White Album' was composed there, its experimental and psychedelic sound a testament to the collective opening of the Fab Four's third eyes under the Maharishi's tutelage. For all of that emphasis on communal positivity, though, a certain rejection of early sixties rock's folk-tinged cheeriness and a dismissal of its 'good vibes' were at work by the end of the decade, as well as a redefining of what 'psychedelic' meant in relation to music. It was becoming less about transforming the world around oneself and more about transcending the limitations of oneself through inner experience and reflection. The cosmic was being pushed aside in favour of the terrestrial. This myopia would welcome a confluence of 'bad vibes' that were welling up in various corners of the world, an explosion of violence and sorrow lurking in the darkness of cultural recesses: the Manson Family was camping out in the California desert, preparing for a race war prophesied by the Beatles themselves (through gross lyrical misinterpretation by Manson) on the 'White Album'; the Japanese Red Army Faction, which included a member of Les Rallizes Denudes, were gearing up to hijack a Japan Airlines Boeing 727 airplane as an act of political terrorism; the beginning of the perplexing and seemingly indiscriminate Zodiac murders in San Francisco, California; and the growing geopolitical turmoil over the war-ravaged quagmire that was Vietnam. By the close of 1970 Brian Jones, Janis Joplin, and Jimi Hendrix would all be dead. The Beatles would be dead by then as well, dissolved in a deep pool of animosity. The 'bad vibes' were inescapable, and the 'White Album' reads as a retrospective harbinger.

When most people think of heavier songs by the Beatles, their minds don't jump to Birthday. I think differently, because it's a total rager. I imagine that September evening in 1968 at Abbey Road Studios when the Beatles recorded it. I imagine a studio awash in marijuana smoke and dim light, with McCartney, Lennon, Harrison, and Starr isolated from each other via necessary sound barriers, building up a backing track to a song that had been hastily written and seemed to have little to no deeper meaning. I imagine Harrison and Starr silently raging over their essentially having been relegated to positions as mere sidemen to serve at the beck and call of McCartney's and Lennon's individual muses, desperate to have their own voices heard, their own instrumental prowess acknowledged, their own songs recorded and made an integral part of the Beatles legacy. I imagine McCartney content with

thoughts of his own genius and superiority, comfortable in the knowledge that he could write any sort of song he wanted to and it would be realized and fawned over; I imagine him marvelling at his own commercial viability, a viability that would serve him well in the coming years, post-Beatles dissolution. But mostly I imagine Lennon fuming, raging at McCartney's simplicity, wishing he could take the master tapes for the track and burn them, committing them to the dustbin of history. I imagine Lennon's growing bitterness toward McCartney, the aura of betrayal he must have felt from his former creative partner, who was fast becoming a piece of the establishment Lennon so resented and fought against. I imagine each Beatle giving it their angry everything on Birthday, pouring out their wrecked hearts through their instruments: Lennon and Harrison's distorted, meandering guitars waging a war for stereo dominance over Starr's breakneck drumming, with all four of them screaming their lungs out on the chorus, knowing the end was just around the corner, that a divide was growing ever-wider betwixt them.

Twelve years after it was recorded, Lennon was asked what he thought of Birthday. 'It's a piece of crap,' was the reply. That vitriolic dismissal of the track speaks to the animus at its heart, to the actual depth of feeling, however bleak, that haunts it. It speaks to the feelings of betrayal and dissatisfaction he felt regarding his old band's legacy, and particularly his feelings toward Paul McCartney, feelings that erupted out in the form of How Do You Sleep? I agree with my father: it really *is* one of the angriest songs I've ever heard. And that anger isn't manufactured. It's absolutely real. I hear that same sort of anger in Birthday: in the lyrics, in the instrumental performances. It's heavy on a psychic level. 'Yes we're going to a party, party,' the lyrics intone. But the party is a massive and total bummer. It's a bummer that's heavy with the weight of so much hurt and anger. Heavy with the weight of dead friendships and artistic disgust. 'We're gonna have a good time,' the lyrics promise. But we won't. We can't. The good times are all in the past, and the past is dead — the final betrayal by time.

Yer Blues

MARK GOODALL

'White is using black men's hearts for white men's lives'

Sandy Huffaker

It's overstated, but it can be argued that blues music is the purest form of musical expression. In its traditional form as an emotional cry of pain or despair, a short cut to the soul, it is at the roots of rock music. As the great American writer Richard Wright stated, millions have 'danced with abandonment and sensuous Joy to jigs that had their birth in suffering'.

The main question raised by Yer Blues is whether the song is a parody or conscious attempt at capturing, in a late 1960s manifestation, the spirit of 'The Blues', the form of music essential to the creation of the Beatles sound. Certainly when this question was raised with Lennon by *Rolling Stone* magazine the former seemed to be paramount and Lennon's answer crystallizes the shame felt by white English musicians in adopting the music of poor black Americans:

'I'm a bit self-conscious — we all were a bit self-conscious and the Beatles were

super self-conscious people about parody of Americans which we do and have done. I know we developed our own style but we still in a way parodied American music.'

There was a sense in which this self-consciousness needed to be reflected in the title of the song. Instead of a 'Blues' it becomes Yer Blues a kind of Scouse inflection added to diminish the seriousness of the song. McCartney was keen to rock out unselfconsciously: 'Don't call it Yer Blues just say it straight', he is reported to have said. Lennon however was uncharacteristically unsure: 'I was self-conscious and I went for "Yer Blues". I think all that has passed now, because all the musicians... we've all gotten over it. That's self-consciousness'.

As always, it is interesting to compare the acoustic demo version of the song with the published version. In the 'Esher' version the blues inflections are subtler, softer. For the final LP version the song has been transformed into a harsh, brutal cry of pain. The electric guitars are harsh and raw with very little in the way of effects added; the bass rumbles menacingly; the drums are a relentless wash of crash cymbal, while the vocal becomes a howl of despair. The Beatley 'whoos' in the demo are gone. A harsh edit near the end, crudely cutting in a different take of the song,

only exacerbates the discomfort. The blues expressed in the song is therefore very physical, from the basic production of the musical backing to the screaming vocals that express real agony. Perhaps the transportation of the song from a relaxed meditative 'hippy' context to the glare of the modern day recording studio and the abrasive egos of musicians, producers and engineers forced a more violent performance?

Either way, for the Beatles the blues was always an expression of this truth. Lennon again:

'In the early days in England, all the groups were like Elvis and a backing group, and the Beatles deliberately didn't move like Elvis. That was our policy because we found it stupid and bullshit. Then Mick Jagger came out and resurrected "bullshit movement," wiggling your arse. So then people began to say the Beatles were passé because they don't move. But we did it as a conscious move.'

Through Lennon's voice, Yer Blues expresses the 'submerged theme of guilt, psychological in nature' that Wright characterizes as the Blues' most striking feature. Similarly, Lennon, perhaps better than any other 1960s pop singer, was able to express the 'masochism' and yet also the 'sensuality' Wright speaks of as being essential to the form without pretension or self-indulgence (see Jagger again for an example of the opposite of this). It is the 'pain of separation and loneliness' as opposed to the sexual dimension of blues expression that comes through.

'White folk singing the blues' can only ever be a representation of the true spirit of black suffering, although it of course is still immensely powerful and expressive. As Wright says, 'In every large city of the earth where lonely, disinherited men congregate for pleasure or amusement, the orgiastic wail of the blues, and their strident offspring, jazz, can be heard'. It's not absurd to claim Liverpool, that 'terrible city where the main street is the ocean' (Malcolm Lowry), can be counted as such a place.

We see in this rock music a strain of blues that was a diversion from the other significant move blues took, through modern jazz — what LeRoi Jones calls the 'cool style'. The blues of Yer Blues can be read as a 'kind of spontaneous intuitive critical method', the kind of free expression that Lennon loved to work out of.

The Beatles LP can be seen as a true expression of what the individual group members were experiencing in that period following the death of Brian Epstein and the flowering of individualistic lives and career paths. And Yer Blues is a notable contribution to the lexicon of suffering expressed through musical sound.

Mother Nature's Son

MATT JONES

As McCartney picks his way through the first verse of Mother Nature's Son somewhere in the shadows of Abbey Road on an August afternoon in 1968, you can almost hear his generation packing their suitcases, donning highly impractical city clothing, and purchasing ordnance survey maps in newsagents' as they head off to the countryside to pay their dues to nature. There would be no better song to have ringing in your ears as you abandoned Ladbroke Grove and sallied forth to Wales, 'to get your head together.' If hippy culture had reached its zenith the previous year, then the world outside and inside Abbey Road studios and McCartney's head that August day in 1968 was a place, as the saying goes, of 'seismic social change'. Things were getting serious: students rioting outside the Sorbonne, John Carlos and Tommie Smith (the American athlete, not the Liverpudlian footballer) raising a black glove of defiance during the medal ceremony for the 200-metre sprint at the Mexico Olympics, and of course the devastating establishment backlash as 'the Man' fought back. Oh to be in England — or Berkeley, or Paris — during the summer of '68 with the whiff of social unrest in the air, the possibility of social change in the offing, and the sound of Mother Nature's Son still ringing in your ears as you stopped off for twenty Players No.6 at the *siop-y-pentre* in Dolgellau where nobody spoke English, on your way to conquer Snowdon in a skimpy nylon mackintosh and a pair of leaky slip-ons.

The thing is you *can* go back there if you like. All you need — *all you need* — is to listen to this song. It didn't occur to me when I first heard it in 1978, ten years after that fateful August day at Abbey Road — post-Wilson, post-Heath, with Thatcher donning her helmet and wings in preparation for the Finch-

ley Players' staging of Wagner's *The Ring of the Nibeling* — that it's just McCartney playing. And it doesn't matter to me now that I know it's just him and not the whole band. Nor could I care one jot that Weller wrote and played English Rose all by himself on *All Mod Cons*, a 1978 release that bears comparison with the 'White Album', shifting gears like James Hunt in a Marlborough McClaren. I can tell — without picking up my guitar — that it's in the key of D. That's the best key of all for singing someone's praises, for paying homage, quietly or noisily, whispering or screaming. I couldn't put my guitar down in 1978 amidst all these enchantments. In fact, the first thing I do when I hear it now is sit down and reacquaint myself with the beautiful chord sequence, humming George Martin's brass-band arrangement and imagining the timpani — all the elements which together make this a triumphal procession from the city to the countryside.

Later on, I might write a song, and if I do it will be an *homage*: not to the countryside but to songs like Mother Nature's Son. If you haven't got the train fare or the bus money or the inappropriate clothing then you can always listen to the song instead. It'll be just as good.

Everybody's Got Something to Hide Except Me and My Monkey

RICHARD MILLS

Everybody's Got Something To Hide Except For Me And My Monkey is a minor footnote in the Beatles canon. However, it is an important song because like many of the songs on the 'White Album' (Dear Prudence, Sexy Sadie, Mother Nature's Son) it was informed by the Beatles' involvement with the Maharishi Mahesh Yogi and his philosophy of Transcendental Meditation. The Beatles spent 1967 and 1968 preoccupied with Transcendental Meditation: they attended a lecture by the Maharishi at the Hilton Hotel, Park Lane, London on 24 August 1967, they spent a long weekend in at the Maharishi's 'Spiritual Regeneration' seminar, Bangor, North Wales 27 August 1967 and from February 1968 to April 1968 the four Beatles intermittently sought enlightenment at his ashram in Rishikesh, India.

The Maharishi's philosophy promulgated Yogic flying, dematerialisations and enlightenment for its adherents. The Beatles were heavily involved in this quest for spiritual enlightenment: A practical and down-to-earth McCartney felt that it was a 'System of relaxation, noting more!' Harrison retained a lifelong fascination with Hinduist philosophy. After his first encounter with yoga, the sitar and mediation, he stated 'I felt I wanted to walk out of my home that day and take a one-way ticket to Calcutta'. Starr famously only spent ten days in Rishikesk likening it to Butlin's holiday camp, but the effect was long lasting and as late as 1987 on the Michael Aspel chat show when asked about the Maharishi, he said he 'believed in God'.

John Lennon's attitude to the Maharishi is the most fascinating, and Everybody's Got Something To Hide Except For Me And My Monkey is a track that reveals his contradictory feelings towards the Maharishi's teachings: the song's lyric 'Come on and feel the joy' is underscored by secular hard rock and bluesy stylings; 'Musically, it marks a further stage in the post-psychedelic re-emergence of Lennon, the rock and roller'. (MacDonald, 2008: 293)[1]

David Quantick captures Lennon's ambivalence in the song:

> There's an often-repeated story of Lennon going up in a helicopter with the Maharishi in the belief that, when they were alone together, the Yogi might 'slip him the answer'. Cynicism and naivety often being different sides of one coin, it's easy to see how Lennon's excitement at the prospect of being shown something fresh, pure, and innocent could flip over into disgust and contempt when that something turned out to be apparently corrupt.

The song's lyrics express Lennon's optimism about Hinduism, and the upbeat violent music his anger. In fact, his disillusionment was so strong that after the hippy dream was over and sixties idealism had ebbed way, Lennon's feelings on the Maharishi were captured in a *Rolling Stone* interview in 1970, when discussing Brian Epstein's death:

> 'Somebody came up to us — the press were there because we'd gone down with this strange Indian. And they said, "Brian's dead." I was stunned. We all were. And the

Maharishi — we went into him, "He's dead and all that. And he was sort of saying, "Oh forget it, be happy". Fucking idiot.'

Another of the most memorable interviews with Lennon in Bangor, North Wales, took place on the 27 August 1967. The Beatles were attending a ten-day Transcendental Meditation with the Maharishi Mahesh Yogi course at Bangor University and John Lennon is interviewed by the BBC, having just heard about the death of Brian Epstein. The interview is so striking because it reveals a traumatised Lennon ventriloquizing the Maharishi's mystical platitudes to the media sharks. Lennon in this clip is visibly shocked, his eyes roll disconsolately in his head, he constantly licks his lips, his voice is nasal and robotic and when he does manage a sentence he trots out Hindu aphorisms on bliss, joy and happiness, as if reading from an autocue: 'Whatever thoughts we have of Brian to keep them happy because any thoughts we have of him will travel to him wherever he is'.

In a sense, this interview of a pasty, moon-eyed Lennon dressed in psychedelic clothes and hippy beads, reveals a confused mind that instinctively clutches at vague and mundane ideas in an attempt to repress grief and anguish. Similarly the song Every-

---

1 MacDonald, I. (2008), *Revolution in the Head: The Beatles' Records and the Sixties*, 216–7, London: Vintage.

body's Got Something To Hide Except For Me And My Monkey is a text which reveals a chaotic mind trying to find equilibrium in a Hindu/Hippy refrain. Lennon sings in the song 'Come on and feel the joy', desperately trying to hide doubt, fear and a mess of contradictory impulses behind a joyful, yet frustratingly unsatisfying mantra. The song has another chant: 'The deeper you go / The higher you fly / The higher you fly / The deeper you go.' According to George Harrison it was 'A saying of the Maharishi' that Lennon lifted verbatim and turned into a song and repeated in a cathartic attempt at bliss. However, the mystical and ethereal lyrics are in conflict with the bluesy guitar lick of E/A/B7/D/G: an earthy counterpoint to the fey Eastern mysticism of the lyrics. This conflict between the joyful Maharishi inspired lyrics and its terse musical accompaniment captures Lennon's disillusionment with the Maharishi's teachings. The refrains are not joyful, especially when coupled with the lyric's connoting heroin addiction (McCartney believes that the title comes from jazz slang for heroin, 'monkey' on my back).

An alternative theory is for the use of the word 'monkey' is that 'Lennon had recently been piqued by a cartoon that portrayed Yoko as a monkey clinging to her Beatle lover's back and took "monkey" as his pet name for Ono'. The song entreats the listener to feel the joy, but the lyrics also hint a more troubled mind, a befuddled psyche: 'Whenever I meditate, there's a big brass band in me head [...] Although it was very beautiful and I was meditating about eight hours a day, I was writing the most miserable songs on earth'. The lyrics 'Your inside is out when your outside is in / Your outside is in when your inside is out' are a typical paradox that hints at a fractured mind: they are jumbled words that invert sense showing Lennon's trauma at alienating global fame, his mother's death and an emotional black hole that the Maharishi's Spiritual Regeneration Movement couldn't salve.

These surrealist words express a similar mental exhaustion and confusion to verse six of Strawberry Fields Forever, where sense breaks down completely. Ian MacDonald suggests that this 'theme of sensations too confusing, intense, or personal to articulate' recurs through his work often showing 'creative inarticulacy reflected in the halting childlike quality of his lyric'. These befogged words give an insight into a man who has suffered a nervous breakdown and who will latch on to any philosophical panacea to obtain peace of mind. But the garbled lyrics are only half the story: this song represents Lennon using performance as catharsis, and the song captures the moment when his interest in the Maharishi was turning to bitterness, anger and resentment towards all grand narratives (Christianity, Buddhism, Hinduism and Marxism). So the angry brio and the élan of frantic guitar, the berserk handbells and all four Beatles clapping manically captures Lennon enshrining his aguish into a rowdy rock song that has 'routinized in a methodology or style […] compulsive repetition, including the compulsively repetitive turn to aporia, paradox, or impasse'. This is the key to the song, Hinduist blissful lyrics which are in direct contrast to the raucous howl of the brainsick music. The confessional angst of track prefigures the angry idolatry of Lennon's Cold Turkey from the *Plastic Ono Band* (1970), a song which tears down Lennon's idols.

Everybody's Got Something To Hide Except For Me And My Monkey forms a suite of songs on the 'White Album' which are about disillusionment with Transcendental Meditation and which express Lennon's psychological pain. The most famous denunciation of the Spiritual Regeneration Movement is Sexy Sadie, a song originally entitled Maharishi, and which in an outtake, refers to his holiness in a four-letter Germanic word; Yer Blues, written in Rishikesh and 'about trying to find God and feeling suicidal'; and Happiness is a Warm Gun, which ranges from

'irony, through self-destructive despair, and obscurely renewed energy to a finale that wrests exhausted fulfilment from anguish'. The Beatles' engineer, Geoff Emerick, describes the collective mind-set of the Beatles during the 'White Album' sessions:

> *'They had come back from India completely different people. They had once been fastidious and fashionable, now they were scruffy and unkempt. They had once been witty and full of humour; now they were solemn and prickly. They had once bonded together as lifelong friends; now they resented each other's company. They were once light-hearted and fun to be around. Now they were angry.'*

Everybody's Got Something To Hide captures this tension. It is a Janus-faced song, the lyrics looking back to a golden blissful summer high in the foothills of the Himalayas before disillusionment with the Maharishi set in, and the music looking forward to Lennon's angry deconstructive rants against the world in his first solo album, *John Lennon/ Plastic Ono Band*. It is a song which reveals a tumultuous mind in flux.

Everybody's Got Something To Hide Except For Me And My Monkey is a text which reveals the chaotic and traumatised psychology of its writer John Lennon. It is a song which shows that the Beatles' interest in Hinduism, and the Maharishi's brand of Transcendental Meditation, ranged from love (Harrison) to hate (Lennon) and that Indian culture resonated a deep, nuanced and revolutionary influence on all four Beatles, and on western culture.

It seems that the band's trip to India affected the world to a great degree by the end of 1968, courses on yoga and on vegetarian cooking were flourishing, mediation centres had opened across the United States and Europe. [...] They definitely popularised Ravi Shankar's music, and paved the way for Indian musical tradition in the West. (Kocot, 2001: 195)[1]

On a personal level, John, Paul, George and Ringo's interest ebbed and flowed, but never entirely dissipated, and this song buried deep on the 'White Album' captures the contradictions the Beatles felt towards the Maharishi. In the last interview before his death, Lennon's words are peppered with references to mysticism, and the word cosmic, and references to Buddha recur throughout (BBC, 1980). After Linda McCartney's death,

McCartney (the man who had referred to the giggling guru as a 'funny bloke') visited the Maharishi at his Global Country of World Peace in Vlodrop, south-eastern Holland seeking spiritual solace from the non-materialistic holy man, who now boasted a Transcendental Meditation empire reputedly worth £600 million. Harrison was chanting to his death and his last album *Brainwashed* (2001) ended with a Hindu mantra. And Ringo Starr played a benefit concert to promote the Transcendental Meditation programme in schools at Radio City Music Hall, New York in 2009. So, although Lennon was often nasty and cynical about the Maharishi and his teachings; all four Beatles would find that his influence cast a long shadow over their post-Beatles careers.

Everybody's Got Something To Hide Except Me And Monkey demonstrates that the Beatles' fascination with the Maharishi Mahesh Yogi and meditation was a serious attempt to fly the mist nets of a shallow, materialistic rock culture and to find deep primordial truths; however, the earthy cynicism and blues figures of the song are prescient, ringing warning bells of disillusionment, as Transcendental Meditation ultimately proved to be a mundane, materialistic and empty labyrinth above which the Beatles could not soar.

1 Kocot, M. (2010), *Fifty Years with The Beatles: The Impact of the Beatles on Contemporary Culture*, 195, Lodz: University of Lodz Press.

Sexy Sadie

BLUE-JOHN BENJAMIN

Malum Discordiæ

Paradise entered its decline
In nineteen sixty-eight
(Which sparked Lennon's song à clef) –
Beyond a void left by pills and wine,
Scoring the protégés' fruitless wait.

Until the saddening rot set in,
Sweet Sadie put on many an arty,
Psychonautical garden party —
A hip Sally Army vibe sort of thing,
Suffused with nectar; no one got arsey.

Then came the tear gas; the jus de citron;
A tainted apple; a swollen LP
(A ruddy great mishmash, if you ask me);
Painted ladies trampled on;
An end to the idyll under the sea.

Thus sunlight was seldom darker than
In the heat of sixty-eight
(*Love, love, love* for Sadie switc to hate) —
Beyond the death of a brilliant man
And the Beatles' last retreat.

Helter Skelter

JAMES RILEY

In 1988 U2 released their concert film *Rattle and Hum*. Shot in moody black and white by Phil Joanou, the film covers the North American leg of the band's 1987 world tour in support of their commercially successful fifth album *The Joshua Tree* (1987). Although it features some scenes shot in Dublin, the film, like the album it documents, fixates upon a particular idea of America; one that's ostensibly 'rootsy' and in thrall to the open spaces of nineteenth century frontier myths but at the same time is, despite itself, utterly indicative of the country's confused and chaotic status in the latter years of the twentieth century.

In a precredit sequence Joanou introduces the band on-stage before using a classic reverse angle à la *The Song Remains the Same* (1976) to reveal the amassed stadium audience. During this set up U2 are pictured in full shamanic mode (that is, they come across like a pantomime version of The Doors) as they plod through a workmanlike cover of Helter Skelter (1968) by the Beatles. An Irish band dressed as biker-cowboys

singing a song by a defunct English group doesn't immediately sit well with the alleged aim of *Rattle and Hum* to examine American culture. However it's Bono's strange on-stage introduction to the song that reminds us just how closely it is connected to a particularly dark aspect of the American psyche. 'This is a song Charles Manson stole from the Beatles,' he announces in the first words of the film, 'we're stealing it back.'

How do you steal a song, especially a song by such as well-known group as the Beatles? U2's version certainly wasn't the first cover of Helter Skelter by a major mainstream band. It follows on from and is no different to the covers performed by Aerosmith in 1975 and Motley Crüe in 1983. However much *Rattle and Hum* works as a smug act of cultural appropriation, there's clearly no plagiarism involved in U2 choosing to perform the track. Much the same can be said of Charles Manson, the alleged 'thief' in this instance. By the time U2 were playing in Denver's McNichols Sports Arena on 8th November 1987, Manson was at Vacaville prison, California, entering his seventeenth year of incarceration for his role in the Tate-La Bianca murders of August 8th–9th, 1969. During that time a number of albums had appeared under his name. Apart from a brief, ghostly recitation apparently recorded in his cell, Manson's discography is not known to include a version of the Lennon-McCartney song.

Although Helter Skelter has become synonymous with Manson, the link between the two far exceeds the imitative work of a cover version. To speak of this connection as 'theft' is inaccurate because Manson did not merely claim the song as his own. Instead, he made Helter Skelter *mean* something very specific within the micro-climate of the 'family'. Add to this the proliferation of a Manson culture industry in the years following 1969 and one finds Helter Skelter labelling books, films and other media that further distances the term from *The Beatles* (1968). The phrase now carries a resonance that ties it more to Spahn Ranch than to Abbey Road. This is the connection exploited by Skinny Puppy in Worlock (1987) and, consciously or not, it's the same wavelength that U2 tune into via their attempt to steal Helter Skelter 'back'.

Helter Skelter is the sixth track on side three of *The Beatles*. Recorded over the course of two extended sessions on 18th July 1968 and 9th September 1968, it is purported to be McCartney's attempt to write something of an anti-ballad. Repeatedly praised by fans of hard rock as prototypical metal, the song is equally derided by some Beatles aficionados as the discordant anomaly. But set it alongside Revolution Number 9 and to a lesser extent, Back In The U.S.S.R., to say nothing of Happiness Is A Warm Gun and that other Manson favourite, Piggies and you do start to see a consistency which befits the album as a whole. You could argue that it's actually ditties like Honey Pie that have no place amongst this strategically discordant set of songs. *The Beatles*, much more so than *Revolver* (1966) or *Sgt. Pepper* (1967) is an album of socio-political cacophony backed by the appropriate sonic accompaniment: tape-delay, echo, amplified drums and reverb. It speaks more of the band members' extracurricular activities like Carnival of Light (1967), *Electronic Sound* (1969) and *Unfinished Music no.1* (1969), than it does the albums that would follow, *Abbey Road* (1969) and *Let It Be* (1970). By the same token, Helter Skelter is not the 'first' metal song, nor is it the anti-Beatles song. It's just as melodic as all their others and only really departs from, say, Paperback Writer (1966) in terms of volume and tempo. As for proto-metal, I reckon Blue Cheer have more claim to that, if not The Brave New World. No: the force of Helter Skelter has very little to do with its alleged difference from the rest of the material on *The Beatles*. Rather, its dissonance comes from its role in the wider myth of the Beatles as a band.

Like it or not the Beatles encapsulate a particular image of Britain in the 1960s. Fitting perfectly within the decade's brackets, their ten-year narrative 1960–1970, speaks of cheeky Liverpudlians on the make, rapid wealth, psychedelic exploration before a *Prisoner*-esque fall-out of frustrated creativity, business rancour and a bad rooftop gig. They all look tired and depressed in that footage by Michael Lindsay-Hogg. The 'concert' is basically one interminable jam of Get Back that's for the most part muddied by the breeze. It's a grey lunchtime and no one seems to be having any fun, least of all the workers of Saville Row who, after clamouring to get a view from the opposite office, just seem to stand there as if waiting for the Apple building to collapse. Then the police come marching in and not long after that John Lennon is playing live in Toronto with Yoko Ono and she's rolling around the stage, in a bag.

If the Beatles work as a convenient metonym for the social mobility, enterprise and affluence commonly associated with 1960s Britain, their break up is one of many indices that commonly name the end of the sixties. The first is a flimsy historiographic reading, the second is an equally flimsy cultural reading; flimsy but nevertheless persistent. Applied to the British experience, the end of the sixties describes the apparent eclipse during the postwar period of the socio-economic prestige the nation had enjoyed under the banner *Pax Brittania*. In this respect it is Helter Skelter, with its imagery of rise and fall that provides a possible soundtrack not just for the collapse of the Beatles, but of this wider sense of British decline. McCartney said as much when explaining the song's terminal implications to Barry Miles. He described Helter Skelter in terms of the 'rise and fall of the Roman Empire' and placed specific emphasis on the notion of 'demise'. Anthony Mann's *The Fall of the Roman Empire* had made the rounds in 1964 and this, combined with the continuing circulation of its source text, Gibbon's *Decline and Fall* (1776–89), helped to establish 'the ruins of Rome' as a tool for understanding the increasingly de-colonised, post-Suez state of the British 'Empire'. That said, when considering McCartney's lyrics it's difficult to make the leap from lovers, not dancers to a deeply metaphorical historical trope pertaining to the loss of imperial hegemony. This is because the song is already built around an existing metaphor, albeit one that is strangely inverted.

McCartney uses the image of a slide in the manner of the typical funfair helter-skelter to create the song's central motif of a repeated, spiral descent. From here, the act of 'coming down fast' adds a sense of vertigo as if the movement is simultaneously a fall, intentional or not. That this downward motion is repeated throughout the song, as if part of a Sisyphean cycle, adds weight to the slide's role as a symbol of a wider sense of confusion, if not chaos. The scene contained in the lyrics, although sparsely sketched, is one that's never at rest. There's a constant refrain of velocity and descent, ideas that can easily be recast in general terms as a 'rapid decline'. But in getting the *slide* to connote tumbling, falling and confusion, McCartney is actually getting things back to front. The term 'helter-skelter' is an adverb originally meaning 'a jingling expression vaguely imitating the hurried clatter of feet'. In this respect the meaning of the phrase is virtually indistinguishable from 'hurry-scurry', 'harum-scarum' and a number of similar sounding colloquialisms. Eventually, 'helter-skelter' came to define movement characterized by 'disorderly haste or headlong confusion,' hence, the idea of a 'helter-skelter run or flight'. What

appeared at the Hull Fair in October 1905 was a Helter Skelter slide because plunging down the spiral on a burlap mat could best be described as 'disorderly haste'. Thus, when we use 'helter-skelter' as a noun, it's a metaphorical extension of this much earlier term for confusion, not the other way round. Placed within McCartney's song, his lyrics then become oddly self-reinforcing. All one gets is a sense of confusion and disorder, not a set of symbols that stand-in for ideas external to the song. Whereas Back In The U.S.S.R. sets out to cite the Beach Boys, Helter Skelter has no such reference point in mind. Certainly if we accept the account that the song emerged out of a desire to create a loud, 'wild' track, it connotes nothing but its own statements and sonic explorations of 'headlong confusion'. As a result, the possible lines of interpretation are legion: the decline of the Beatles, the decline of society, the loss of empire, whatever. It could mean anything. Which is why it became so attractive to Charles Manson.

It's unlikely that Manson was a devotee of traditional English fairground rides. Instead, he felt that he shared the same psychic space as the Beatles and they were using their music to communicate with him directly. According to Vincent Bugliosi, Manson first heard The Beatles in December 1968, just after its release. By the end of the year his followers were listening to the album repeatedly as one way of 'preparing' for the events he came to call Helter Skelter. What Manson got from the song was a distillation of one of his abiding concerns, that of imminent societal breakdown. But Manson was not merely a survivalist. He saw this process as a necessary part of his own messianic narrative. Whether he believed his pitch or not the outline, unfolded to Bugliosi during the trial proceedings, went as follows. The modus operandi of the 'family' was to incite an apocalyptic race war between black and white America. They would do this by committing atrocious acts of murder in the homes of affluent white people leaving suggestive evidence that the perpetrators were black. In the ensuing street battles and general chaos as decades of racial tension and mutual distrust came to the fore, the Manson family would retreat to the desert in their dune buggies and descend to a secret subterranean world. There, in the probable company of the Beatles themselves, the Family would sit-out the destructive black revolution. They would remain hidden until the newly sovereign black nation began to falter in their unfamiliar roles as leaders. At which point Manson, his multiplied disciples and the Beatles would re-emerge from 'the bottomless pit' and assume their rightful place as rulers of the world. Manson used Helter Skelter to name this entire scenario because he saw it as the point at which everything would 'come down'. Presumably this is to be understood on two levels, 'come down' in the sense of fall and collapse and 'come down' in the sense of inheritance.

It goes without saying that this is a problematic narrative and one that's also unconnected to the original song. Bugliosi is right to give the scenario short shrift in his account of the trial. However, the absurdity and offensiveness of the idea didn't stop him from using *Helter Skelter* as the title of his book. If anything has allowed the Manson murders to assume a dubious level of fame, it's this crystallizing phrase. The *Life* cover featuring 'the Love and Terror Cult' may have helped to sell T-shirts, but as Adam Parfrey's collage, 'The Revelation of the Sacred Door' indicates, it's the scrawled presence of 'Helter Skelter' at Spahn Ranch and 'Healter Skelter' at the La Bianca residence that have allowed the case to generate a peculiar iconicity. More so than the Bay Area murders associated with the Zodiac Killer, the Tate-LaBianca case weaves together a number of highly resonant strands: the counterculture, film-stars, apocalypticism and rock music. There are overlaps (co-incidental and not so co-incidental) with Dennis

Wilson of the Beach Boys, Anton LaVey of the Church of Satan and Robert DeGrimston of The Process Church of the Final Judgement. These coincidences of 'geography, money and show-business' are held together by the term 'Helter Skelter'. The phrase simultaneously connects Manson's actions to a specifically Californian end-of-the-world narrative and British rock music of the late-1960s. If we are to see the whole subculture of Charles Manson as a matrix of action, mediation and myth then Helter Skelter understood as song *and* symbol forms the glue that binds these nodal points.

Despite their rescue attempt, it's hard to see U2's cover doing anything but recapitulating this status particularly as their tour and the release of their film bookended two key 'Mansonoid' events. In 1987 Amok Press published *Apocalypse Culture*, a collection of essays edited by Adam Parfrey. The book attempted to analyse the forces 'lurking behind' the 'mass delirium' of the late 20th century, the belief expressed on the part of 'occult prophets, nihilist kids, born agains and liberal humanists' that a 'global catastrophe' was imminent. In August 1988 Parfrey, along with Anton LaVey, Boyd Rice and Nikolas Schreck appeared at the '8/8/88 Rally', a concert and 'Satanic' gathering that included Parfrey, Anton LaVey and a screen-ing of Frank Howard's Manson film *The Other Side of Madness* (1970).

Apocalypse Culture opens with Latter Day Lycanthropy, Parfey's essay on the struggle to either repress or release 'the animal in man' and the late-twentieth century shift towards the latter in art and culture. Parfrey includes Nick Bougas' illustration of a lycanthropic Charles Manson and quotes the 'manifesto' of Radio Werewolf, a performance group led by Schreck that 'celebrates the lunar force of animist apocalypse as a reaction against directionless humanity'. The implication is that Manson acts as an exemplary figure of amoral misanthropy. He exhibits the necessary 'psychic preparation for the millennial calamities which are thought to lie ahead'. Radio Werewolf performed at the 8/8/88 concert which was designed as a 'reaffirmation of the "riding forth" ritual conducted on the eve of the Tate murders in 1969'. The event thus seems to develop the image of Manson from that of celebrated misanthrope into an emblem of an almost archetypal 'force' of violence. By extension, the lycanthropic theory that *Apocalypse Culture* outlines is extended into the weird status of the event, oscillating somewhere between ritual and actualization. The idea of 'reaffirmation' conveys a sense of both commemoration and repetition as if to point to the memorialization of a previous act of violence as well as its reactivation through violence yet to come.

Staring out into the stadium crowd, with the vast imaginary spaces of America before them, U2 must have thought something similar as they began to ride fourth. They talk of feeling 'confusion' whilst on tour, but it's clear from the surrounding cultural context that they're not the only ones in Reagan-era America to experience intense fear and loathing. That these seemingly disparate parties each draw upon a shared set of references to express their parallel anxieties speaks volumes about this weird Beatles song from 1968. Helter Skelter is extremely generous with its symbolism. It does for the immediate post-Beatles era what *Fight Club* would do for the millennial turn. Whether you're mired in first-world ennui or waiting for the apocalypse, the song provides a catch-all label to describe the feeling that 'it' is coming down fast.

Long, Long, Long

MARK GOODALL

A seemingly inconsequential track on the 'White Album', Long, Long, Long grows with repeat listening into a hauntingly beautiful paean to the search for religious belief or romantic love; the composition another sign of composer George Harrison's growing devotion to spiritual enlightenment. A curious structure incorporates a soft plaintive finger-picked acoustic guitar opening with gentle organ chords (resonant of the folk-rock scene developing around the time of the late 1960s) leading to a surging, pleading bridge and ending with an avant-garde mish-mash of ambient noise, scraped guitar strings, 'proggy' organ chords, anguished cries, drums and the sound of a bottle of Blue Nun wine rattling on top of the organ cabinet. The creative, improvised decision to end a pastoral and lyrical song with a burst of disquieting death-like noise seems typical of the group's desire to counterbalance seriousness with humour and subversion, reconciliation with the occult. Long, Long, Long is the Beatles interest in 'heavy conscious creation' writ large (or small).

An interesting detail to the song is revealed in Mark Lewisohn's *The Complete Beatles Recording Sessions* when it is mentioned that sessions for the 'White Album' were created against the pungent background of Durbar incense sticks sourced from India. We are used to the many photographic records of the group at work in the studio, and latterly on film with *Let It Be*. But here a sense is thus evoked of the *smell* of the Beatles at work, the almost overwhelming odour of the incense generating a special atmosphere for creative production. Not everyone was a fan of the Durbar sticks. As recording engineer Richard Lush reveals, 'the people at Abbey Road didn't particularly like them'.

Revolution 1

DAVID OWEN

Gil Scott-Heron was wrong.

The revolution WILL be televised.

On Demand. Pay per view. Live streaming.

With commercial breaks, adverts and sponsors.

Available across all devices.

It's trending on Twitter.

Running riot in Nike trainers.

Product placement. Designer petrol bombs.

Revolution and dissent will be commodities. Lifestyle choices.

Thomas Frank was right.

There's money to be made fighting "the man".

Honey Pie

DAVID E. WILLIAMS

Conventional wisdom dictates that so-called rebellion is the indispensable element in rock and roll. Prior to any discussion of chords and beats, there is always the image of Elvis' swagger, Jagger's sneer or Rotten's snarl. For half a century now, tales of bad boys and badass girls have fueled the marketing plans of the latest artists 'on the edge'.

Did you know Jim Morrison had an asthmatic brother and used to scotch tape his mouth shut while he slept? Google it. I just did. I couldn't find the story. But I guarantee I heard it once, and for the sake of argument, isn't that enough? In rock and roll, fake news is nothing new. Or even fake.

Against this backdrop, we consider McCartney. He's the tops of course. He's the Eiffel Tower. You don't get any more rock and roll than putting notes together in a psychic configuration accidentally inciting mass murder. I mean, 'oops!' And it's some goofy ass song about a rollercoaster or something.

Still, though… goody fucking two shoes, right?

Yes, actually.

While John Lennon was a plucky misbehaver (though perhaps not as naughty as Morrison!), those who have read or seen any Beatles biography recall the image of adolescent Paul at the family piano, cranking out the hits of British music hall to his loving relations.

It was a musical family. Although Paul's father, Jim, had a lifelong day job in the textile industry, he played in a ragtime band in his twenties known as the Masked Melody Makers (named for the novelty black masks they wore while performing). He wrote a song for the band called Eloise, which his successful son Paul recorded five decades later as Walking In The Park With Eloise, with Floyd Cramer and Chet Atkins in a one-off project called The Country Hams.

The older Jim McCartney limited his musical exploits to collecting old 78s and playing the parlour piano at family get-togethers. In this manner, young Paul was instilled with a love of jazz and pop and learned the basics of vocal harmony. He also sat down and started playing the darned thing himself.

When he was sixteen, Paul McCartney wrote When I'm Sixty Four on that family piano. He would later discover Elvis, the Mississippi Delta and all the rest of it, even Stockhausen, but unlike so many others to follow, his first inspiration was catchy tunes.

In the liner notes to *Kisses on the Bottom*, Paul writes: 'People will often say "What songs do you like? Who are your favourite composers?" And I say Cole Porter, the Gershwin brothers and people like that, because the songs are very skilled. Cheek To Cheek was always one of my favourite songs.'

John Lennon famously mocked McCartney's contribution to this style as 'Paul's granny songs.' According to Beatles engineer Geoff Emerick, 'granny music shit' is how Lennon once frustratedly referred to Ob La Di, Ob La Da. While they were recording it!

Curiously enough, When I'm Sixty-Four made its way into Beatles' sets as early as their Cavern Club gigs. It was the song they played if the power went out.

Which brings us somehow circuitously to *The Beatles*. Like every Beatles album post *Revolver*, it is argued by some to be their best. Others disagree, opining that four sides is just too long. On this point, McCartney is resolutely opposed. 'Fuck off, it's the Beatles' "White Album",' he has famously stated in a rare impolite outburst. (He does it now and then to keep us thinking he's 'rock and roll,' right? And Kanye West is 'like John Lennon.' Remember, he said *that* too.)

One aspect of the 'White Album' that cannot be denied is that it represents a departure from a pure band dynamic to one of four solo artists playing each other's tunes. Even when all four Beatles are playing, each track more recognizably than previously falls into one of three categories: a Paul song, a John song, a George song. (Sorry… I forgot Don't Pass Me By! OK… FOUR categories: a Paul song, a John song, a George song, a Ringo song.)

Honey Pie — Paul at his most old-fashioned — sits somewhat uncomfortably on the same album side as Revolution No.1 — John at his most radical (not counting his solo material) — and Revolution 9 — the Beatles at their most ludicrously contrived 'avant-garde'.

Lyrically, it's a simple tale of longing. A young North England boy misses a young

North England girl who's crossed the Atlantic to pursue stardom in the USA. It includes the curious admission that 'I'm in love but I'm lazy,' suggesting that our hero envies the girlfriend's pursuit of her dream while he lives out the simple life.

It's corny as corny comes, but Paul delivers with a nod and a wink: it's not difficult to imagine some Liverpudlian lass feeling this way about *him*, in fact.

Our hero pines for Honey's return. 'Will the wind that blew her boat / Across the sea / Kindly send her sailing back to me?' If this were a Nick Cave song, he might travel cross the Atlantic and hack her to pieces with a meat cleaver. Not on Paul's watch!

The production is impeccably faithful to style, with even the brief addition of vinyl surface noise under one line of lyric to evoke an old 78rpm record. This technique has of course become cliché — kind of like publishing an Instagram photo in monochrome — but in 1968 it was conceptually innovative to shade nostalgically by brushing on a little crackle.

Woodwinds whirl about wonderfully, five saxophones and two clarinets, arranged by George Martin, whose role in the execution of Paul's old-timey vision cannot be understated. Even Lennon can't resist the fun, falling in line with a guitar solo straight out of the Django Reinhardt style book. 'John played a brilliant solo on Honey Pie,' the *Beatles Bible* quotes Harrison in 1987. 'It was one of them where you just close your eyes and happen to hit all the right notes... sounded like a little jazz solo.'

If it seems I've been hard on Lennon here, I'll mitigate with McCartney's recollection that, 'granny shit' comments aside, John was actually a fan of this older style as well. 'Two of John's favourite songs, when I met him, were Close Your Eyes (1933), which is very much of that era, and the other was Little White Lies (1930). Those were the kind of songs that we'd been listening to and that attracted me to him. And I do think they did have quite an influence on us melodically.'

McCartney would enthusiastically revisit this style later in his career, not only in the aforementioned Country Hams, but also with Wings on You Gave Me The Answer, originally appearing on *Venus and Mars*, but also a showstopper on the otherwise heavy rockin' (well, you know) *Wings Over America.* The main hook of 'I love you, and you, you seemed to like me' is straight out of an old movie: some Tin Pan Alley guy sitting at a piano with a legal pad.

Baby's Request from *Back to the Egg* is a slower ballad that comes complete with a World War II-themed video of Paul, Linda and the rest of Wings performing in military khaki to tired British soldiers in the desert.

And, on his requisite old-rock-star-album-of-American-songbook-standards, *Kisses on the Bottom*, McCartney had the audacity to contribute a new song of his own, the haunting My Valentine. Of course, it's tough to disagree with critics and fans who deem it the best song on the album!

In 1998, Paul joined much of British pop and rock royalty on *Twentieth Century Blues, The Songs of Noël Coward*; singing A Room with a View.

When asked about the Beatles in the early sixties, Coward, the quintessential British playwright/songwriter/comedian/fop condemned them as 'bad-mannered little shits who had a certain guileless charm and stayed on mercifully for not too long.' Harsh. Still, when McCartney had a chance to meet Coward around the same time, he scolded the other Beatles for not joining him: 'We can't snub Noël Coward! He's two flights downstairs and he's asked to meet us! He's the grand old dame of British showbusiness and we're the new young things.'

It is easy to deduce: Paul McCartney wanted to be Noël Coward.

But ego is as ego does, and, God love him, these days he's pretty happy being Paul McCartney. Who wouldn't be? As always, even at ten-years-older-than-sixty-four, he's in love, but he's certainly not lazy.

Savoy Truffle

JUSTIN SMITH

In the 1960s my aunt owned a sweet shop and tobacconists in the seaside town where I grew up. Below the shelves of jars labelled Everton Mints, Old English Bullseyes and Coltsfoot Rock, the glass-fronted cabinets were filled with boxes of chocolates and candies under their makers' names: Beeches, Clarnicos, Callard & Bowser, Elizabeth Shaw, Bendicks. But these were exclusive brands for her paying customers. If she was giving a present, it was Macintosh's *Good News* — the popular mixture of milk and plain that aimed to please all. I always received a brown paper bag of cheap sweets when I visited, much to my mother's chagrin: 'Think of your teeth!'

I must have first heard snatches of songs from the 'White Album' when my older brother (who was then at university) brought it home (No. 0127063). I remembered the jaunty Ob-La-Di, Ob-La-Da and the sinister-sounding Savoy Truffle — light and dark. Only in retrospect did I discover that the latter quotes the former in the second of its two bridges. What struck me right away was the urgency of Savoy Truffle's opening electric piano riff and the soaring, siren-like warning guitar phrase over the vocal: 'Creee-me Tangerine and Mon-tel-i-mar', and then the thick, distorted horns full of driving menace.

There was a local hotel called The Montelimar on my walk to school and I rarely passed it thereafter without hearing George Harrison's heavy Liverpudlian four-syllable-beat enunciation in my head. I didn't even realize until later that the song's lyrics were the names of actual chocolates: 'Ginger Sling', 'Coffee Dessert'. And not just any chocolates but 'Yes, you know it's Good News', although some poetic licence was exercised to turn 'Pineapple Treat' into 'Pineapple Heart', and 'Cherry Cream' and 'Apple Tart' are pure invention. Moreover, while Harrison sings 'Montelimar' (from the Provençal town whose local speciality dessert nougat gave its name to the candy), the *Good News* menu used the alternative 'Montelimart' (which in print would have afforded a nice visual rhyme with 'Pineapple Heart'). Another interesting variation is provided in the lyric sheet/poster from the original album where the spelling is 'montelimat'.

In the history of chocolate marketing in the post-rationing era the evocative naming of centres lent ordinary assortments both variety and exoticism — the promise of epicurean luxury delivered with all the linguistic excesses of a Dulux paint chart. The commodification of domestic life in the 1960s was orchestrated by the poetry of advertising. Nothing was merely descriptive; everything had connotations.

In this way, Savoy Truffle is a work of pop art in the tradition of David Hockney's Typhoo Tea packet (*Tea Painting in an Illusionistic Style*, 1961) and Andy Warhol's famous *Campbell's Soup Cans* (1962). It is at once a commentary on the ubiquity and cultural purchase of advertising, and a gesture of comic swagger: I can make art out of the everyday, it says; I can write a nonsense song about the box of chocolates you bought last week. But, as Harrison's autobiography testifies, there was more to it than that. It was also personal.

George Harrison's close friend Eric Clapton had a sweet tooth. Allegedly unable to resist the temptations of a box of chocs, he would devour them systematically once opened. And his teeth suffered as a result. Thus, the song works through the *Good News* menu building to the refrain that warns: 'But you'll have to have them all pulled out after the Savoy Truffle.' The Savoy Truffle, as its name suggests, is the epitome of indulgence. It proves the power of advertising by being, at least for Clapton, irresistible. Others have intuited that the song's first bridge hints at more serious addictions:

> You might not feel it now
> But when the pain cuts through
> You're going to know and how
> The sweat is gonna fill your head
> When it becomes too much, you'll shout
> aloud

Clapton was, by now, a heroin user. But I prefer Jonathan Gould's more literal interpretation: he describes Harrison's searing guitar solo as being 'pitched to the register of a dentist's drill'.

In the second bridge the line 'You know that what you eat you are' was apparently suggested to Harrison by the Beatles' Press Officer Derek Taylor. According to Harrison's autobiography, *I Me Mine*, he and Taylor frequently exchanged comic banter and became keen fans of *Monty Python's Flying Circus* when it was first broadcast on BBC Television on 5 October 1969, almost exactly a year after the Savoy Truffle recording sessions began on 3 October 1968. *You Are What You Eat* was the title of a US countercultural music documentary directed by Barry Feinstein that was released in September 1968. Taylor's friend, Alan Pariser, was the production manager. But the slogan itself (from a 1942 book by the American nutritionist Victor H. Lindlahr) had become revitalised with the new trend in macrobiotic diets. Taylor recalled that it 'was a very hippy thing, "Don't eat meat man, you'll be filled with the adrenaline of frightened animals"'. Here the phrase is no less doom-laden: 'But what is sweet now turns so sour'. Many commentators have linked the lines that follow to tensions between Harrison and his fellow Beatles:

We all know ob-la-di-bla-da
But can you show me where you are

John Lennon took no part in the recording of Savoy Truffle. And both he and Harrison disliked McCartney's jolly piece of kitsch. But here the Beatle trio (augmented by Chris Thomas on keyboards) are tight as a drum. Paul's fluid bass under the saxophones is as expressive as any contemporary work by Jack Bruce or John Entwistle. And Ringo's staccato half-beat fills punctuate the verse/bridge arrangement perfectly. Starr adopts a similar technique between verses in Lennon's Glass Onion — another self-reflexive song (in A minor) that in its ascending scale progressions echoes Savoy Truffle (in E minor) and immediately precedes Ob-La-Di, Ob-La-Da: it is the third track on side one; Savoy Truffle comes third on side four. Nothing is accidental.

Greater serendipity is to be found in a sketch recorded for episode six of the first series of *Monty Python's Flying Circus*, broadcast on 23 November 1969 almost exactly a year after the UK release of the 'White Album'. 'Trade Description Act' is a characteristically surreal response to the passing of the *Trade Descriptions Act* in 1968, taking the poetic naming of confectionery to new depths. Graham Chapman and John Cleese's police hygiene squad inspectors interrogate Terry Jones' smooth-talking chocolatier, Mr. Milton of the Whizzo Chocolate Company, over the novel centres featured in a devilish new assortment including: 'Crunchy Frog', 'Ram's Bladder Cup', 'Cockroach Cluster', 'Anthrax Ripple' and 'Spring Surprise'. The joke was doubtless not lost on George Harrison.

Cry Baby Cry

MIKE KIRKUP

DAVID SHEFF: And 'Cry Baby Cry'?
JOHN LENNON: Not me. A piece of rubbish.

The legendary 'White Album'. We first heard it, crashing and tinkling away, around 1972, when we were about ten-years-old, my friend and I. Borrowed from an older girl over the road, we'd heard albums like *With The Beatles* and *A Hard Day's Night*, but this was the first 'late' Beatles we'd come across; not even *Sgt Pepper's Lonely Hearts Club Band* had entered our universe.

When first listening to the album, as well as being thrilled by the music (particularly hearing tracks like Back in the U.S.S.R. and Helter Skelter for the first time) I certainly remember its dark corners and 'hidden' sounds. The first sense of uneasiness comes at the end of Glass Onion, with its prowling strings, as if moving along the corridor of a dark house, spinning downwards in pitch before the barrelhouse piano of Ob-La-Di, Ob-La-Da comes crashing in. It became a game for us finding these pieces to the album's jigsaw — the ''ey up' before While My Guitar Gently Weeps; the very scouse-sounding 'one more time' from George after Piggies; the high pitched 'thank you' at the end of Ob-La-Di, Ob-La-Da'; a drunken murmur, that sounds like '*Hersum blersum hersum…*' at the end of I'm So Tired, and the sound of tea-cups and voices in the middle of Cry Baby Cry. That song in particular I've always found fascinating, and emblematic of the album as a whole, with its 'deceptive sunshine and mysterious laughter behind half open doors' as Ian Macdonald perfectly describes it.

John Lennon seemed to dismiss the song completely in a 1980 interview (see above quote) even claiming it was McCartney's. It's possible he got the title confused with something else (though it's hard to think what that would be) as it's certainly one of his best and most creative pieces, and stands up against Lucy In The Sky With Diamonds, Strawberry Fields Forever, and I Am The Walrus as an example of his 'nonsense' work, and a fascinating reflection on his childhood reading.

The song was one of the earliest composed for the album; in a conversation with Hunter Davies in early Spring 1968, Lennon states that 'I've got another one here, a few words, I think I got them from an advert "cry baby cry, make your mother buy". I've been playing it over on the piano. I've let it go now. It'll come back if I really want it.' Lennon often was often inspired by fragments from other media; a newspaper story about holes in Blackburn for A Day In The Life; a cornflakes advert for Good Morning, Good Morning.

There's also an interesting point made about the album at this time, when Davies states: '[John and Paul] came back [from India] with an idea for its format — the LP would consist of songs from the soundtrack of a non-existent musical. It was originally going to be called 'Doll's House' [note: not A

Doll's House] — Doll being a girl's name and her house being a house of pleasure where all the people in the fictional musical would congregate. But they found that "Doll's House" had already been used as a title.'

Another childhood connection (a doll's house), and a potential collection of characters to live in it and pass through; Prudence, Honey Pie (and her alter ego Wild Honey Pie), Bungalow Bill, Desmond & Molly Jones, Martha, Julia, Rocky Racoon, Sexy Sadie, some blackbirds and some piggies. Both animal references are also connected to sinister nursery rhymes — Four and Twenty Blackbirds where the birds were baked in a pie and survived (an obvious source for Cry Baby Cry too of course) and This Little Piggy, where the porkers take themselves to market to be sold and eaten in an elaborate suicide pact, eat roast beef (at least it's not bacon!) and go *wee wee wee all the way home'* , whatever the hell that means.

Throughout Cry Baby Cry, Lennon's vocal sounds very tired and unemotional, and almost as if he is in a dream state, repeating the limited melody of the verses like a skipping rhyme. In each one, the same notes are repeated over and over without any change in delivery. The musical backing consists of descending semitones from E minor on

bass, piano and acoustic guitar with each verse gradually taking us down, bar by bar (into Doll's basement?), with a jagged seventh chord crashing in on the fifth bar waking us up from the dream.

We then level out on the G major chord, before we start descending again on the next verse. A circular journey of descent and levelling off, descent and levelling off, like a never-ending Escher staircase... but it does end, quite suddenly, with a wavering 'cryyayy', sung by Lennon with a Bee Gee-like exaggerated vibrato.

But it's not quite the end, as attached to the song is a haunting thirty second refrain from McCartney, another piece of flotsam floating between tracks, with the phrase 'Can you take me back where I came from, brother can you take me back?' repeated with just an acoustic guitar and percussion. It's not on the track listing, but fits perfectly with the previous song, with a longing to be 'taken back', to the past, to childhood. Another, and perhaps the best, piece of buried treasure on the album.

Regarding the lyrics, Lennon brings in a range of childhood and childlike sources and memories with the song. Four and Twenty Blackbirds, where he puts his own slant on the King in his counting house, and the Queen making bread and honey, so his king is 'in the kitchen' and the queen is 'playing piano'.

The references to Lewis Carroll are not perhaps as overt as a song like Lucy in the Sky With Diamonds but the influences are certainly there, with the slightly mad king and queen straight from *Through the Looking Glass*, and having tea reminds us of the Mad Hatter's tea party.

The title has a sense of a lullaby, but again, turned on its head, encouraging the infant not to sleep, but to cry ('cry baby cry, make your mother sigh') and can also refer to a 'cry baby', another childish term used to poke fun at 'soft' children.

The phrase 'she's old enough to know better' is a saying I certainly heard on our street growing up as likely would John (that, or, 'she's no better than she ought to be'), said between gossiping neighbours behind a hand. You can imagine him hearing Mimi discussing someone with a friend in the front room at Mendips... maybe referring to Julia? It also could be a playful reference to McCartney's Your Mother Should Know... better?) as other past Beatles' songs are referenced on the album, such as Fixing A Hole, I Am

The Walrus, Fool On The Hill, and Strawberry Fields Forever in Glass Onion, and Ob-La-Di, Ob-La-Da in Savoy Truffle.

David Quantick calls Cry Baby Cry 'a fine and slightly creepy song, in many ways the centrepiece of the "spooky" 'White Album' songs... an eerie cast of fairy-tale nobility... a group of unseen children', and that chimes with MacDonald's description of 'mysterious laughter from behind half-closed doors'. It's a *haunted* doll's house. The children try to raise the dead with a séance and their voices come 'out of nowhere'; the adult king is picking flowers for his friend who's 'coming to play'; the 'always smiling' duchess, with a fixed grin straight from Conrad Veidt in *The Man Who Laughs*; the queen 'playing piano' for the children sounds innocent enough, but we hear three discordant glissandos in the background which doesn't sound like easy listening.

With its nostalgic nods to children's literature, and its singsong chorus, Cry Baby Cry conjures up the idea of a past childhood perfectly, with picture-book kings and queens, and parties and holidays, and tea and gardens, and flowers and crying babies, and parlours — a nice touch using the name of a room that doesn't even exist anymore in the twenty-first century. Whenever I hear the song, I always see the characters in a large Edwardian house (kitchen, parlour, servants, boys in sailor-suits, girls in flower-print dresses, French windows with sunlight streaming in), and at the end of the song, with the final 'Cryaayyy', the figures fade from view, but the house remains, vacated by the people, but furniture still there, ready for the next crowd of people ready to donate to the National Trust.

Additional Sources

Bettelheim, Bruno (1991) *The Uses of Enchantment: The Meaning and Importance of Fairy Tales* Penguin, London

Carroll, Lewis (1992) *Alice's Adventures in Wonderland and Through the Looking Glass* Oxford Classics, Oxford

Golson, G. Barry (ed) (1982) *The Playboy Interviews with John Lennon & Yoko Ono*, New English Library

'The Postmodern White Album,' Ed Whitely in Inglis, Ian (ed) (2000) *A Thousand Voices: The Beatles, Popular Music and Society* Macmillan, Basingstoke

Lewishon, Mark (2000) *The Complete Beatles Chronicle* Hamlyn, London

Mellers, Wilfred (1973) *Twilight of the Gods: The Beatles in Retrospect* Faber and Faber, London

Riley, Tim (1988) *Tell Me Why: A Beatles Commentary* The Bodley Head, Oxford

40th Anniversary of the 'White Album' (BBC Radio 2, 22nd November 2008)

The Beatles (1968) Apple (remastered version 2009)

The Beatles: *Anthology 3* (1996) Apple

Revolution 9

BOB FISCHER

'**E**very one of them knew that as time went by, they'd get a little bit older and a little bit slower.'

The muttering, easily-pleased residents of a sepia, Old Holborn-tainted retirement home; confused amidst the aspidistra, held in a *Readers' Digest* prison of oxtail soup and BBC2 closedowns.

'Take this brother, may it serve you well.'

A battered broadsword passed from blood-stained hand to trembling, outstretched gauntlet beneath the twisted, ridged contours of an ancient, war-torn yew tree.

'The watusi, the twist.'

A slow, mournful waltz around a haunted, desolate dancehall; the rictus grins and hollow sockets of whirling, skeletal faces pressed together.

Revolution 9 takes me to places; to dark cupboards, locked rooms, angry streets and gothic tombs. It conjures up lost dreams, and it resurrects childhood nightmares.

Long derided by 'real music, man' purists, ostracised from hissy C90 tapes and omitted from shiny, digital playlists alike, this eight-minute sound collage is the ultimate casualty of the modern, systematic de-weirding of the Beatles. It isn't heritage rock; it will never be performed by Paul McCartney on the Pyramid Stage or included in medleys on shiny ITV talent shows. It isn't available to play on a console game with a fake, plastic guitar, and a digitised, white-suited John Lennon peering out from the TV screen, beatified and simpering beneath a scrolling fretboard. It remains the sole Beatles song that is the enemy of the musical establishment; fractured and tortured, unsettling and stark. There are those that would have it removed from the album altogether; just as they'd take Yellow Submarine from *Revolver* or consider *Sgt. Pepper* a stiffer, prouder military force if Within You Without You was mercilessly court-martialled and drummed out from within his ranks.

They're wrong on all counts, for the Beatles' power lies in the eclectic. No other band would attach its name to Love Me Do and Love You To; to Octopus's Garden and I Am The Walrus; to When I'm Sixty-Four and Revolution 9.

Eminent neuroscientists have long since debated the numbers. Most claim that the average human brain generates and experiences somewhere between 15,000–80,000 thoughts in an average day. Psychologist Daniel Kahenman has suggested that the 'psychological present' lasts around three seconds; anything else is either 'past' or 'future'. If, by some nightmarish advance of science, we could gain an aural snapshot of this internal monologue, it would surely sound like Revolution 9; a perpetual, violent collision of emotions, words, phrases; snippets of music and random noises, clanging and clashing, relentless and violent. The fact that the subject of our eavesdropping is clearly the thought processes of the 1968 John Lennon makes it, surely, one of the most intensely personal pieces of work that he ever produced.

It is the perfect summation of the violence and anxieties of the era; the Paris riots, the

Vietnam protests, the assassination of Martin Luther King. It positively simmers with nightmarish paranoia and discordant uncertainty. But it is exclusively Lennon's, too, punctuated by his obsession with — and fear of — the number nine, his recently cemented love for Yoko Ono, his delight in non-sequitur incongruity and archaic idiolect. It is chaos, and noise, and madness; the tortured, shadow-bound pre-dinnertime snooze at the end of an album that Ian MacDonald described perfectly as 'the slow afternoon of the Beatles' career'.

'Number Nine. Number Nine. Number Nine.'

The sound of inspiration, of dreamlike creativity, and, ironically, the death knell for a band whose potential for artistic endeavour sadly reached its zenith at the very moment it tore them apart.

Good Night

CHRISTOPHER FOX

Even by the contrary standards of the 'White Album' this is an odd track: a lullaby so sweet that it must surely be by McCartney, yet was actually written by Lennon; the only song on the 'White Album' not sung by its author; a recording on which none of the Beatles appears as an instrumentalist; a marriage of Ringo's characteristically artless singing with the most conventionally artful vocal and instrumental arrangements on any Beatles album. Why is it here? What does its presence tell us about the Beatles in 1968, the confidence they felt in their boundlessly eclectic creativity? But before that, what does it say about me that I have chosen to write about Good Night, a song described by Jonathan Gould as a 'warm tub of bathos', a song which might be 'charitably described as a spoof', a song which leaves one with a feeling of 'banality and sadness'?

When the 'White Album' was released I had decisively shifted my pop allegiances to the Rolling Stones. My cousins Liz and Jerry had already established that Beatles or Stones was a binary divide and Jerry had also established, mostly by having a motor-bike and being at art school, that it was much cooler to be a Stones fan. So I didn't buy the 'White Album' and my Beatles-related activity of the period mostly consisted of explaining to my younger sister why *Sgt. Pepper*, the only Beatles album in our house and one of her treasured possessions, was rubbish.

Indeed my anti-Beatles stance was so hard-line that it was not until two decades later that I started to listen more carefully to their post-*Pepper* output and it took the publication of Ian MacDonald's *Revolution in the Head* to push me into full-blown Fab Four fandom. Did I even hear the tracks on the 'White Album' which weren't singles? I think not. This is not something of which I am particularly proud but it is also not, I think, untypical for people of a certain age. The Beatles were too famous, too poppy, too everywhere, to be taken seriously. Yet there was also the paradox that *Sgt. Pepper* had been taken so seriously — too seriously, of course — and then been followed by a double album whose track listing looked like a jumble sale.

For the last ten years, however, I have lived in a house which contains a vinyl 'White Album', issue No. 0083066 to be precise, and it is for my Beatles-loving Susan, whose LP it has been since 1968, that I am writing about

this song. Another paradox, however: when I told Susan that the editor of this volume had suggested that I bring my classical music sensibilities to bear on one of the more 'classical' tracks, and that I had chosen Good Night, she couldn't at first call it to mind. This in turn may well be indicative of even the most avid fan's response to the 'White Album'. Confronted by so much music, and so much different music, many listeners, especially in the digital age when the next track is just a click away, will skip through from favourite to favourite and, having reached Revolution No.1, may go on to Savoy Truffle, possibly even Cry Baby Cry, but will probably give up on Revolution 9, forgetting that there is still one more track to go.

In our current download-driven world there is often nostalgic talk about the art of LP sequencing, the musical guile which drew listeners from the edge to the centre of a record and encouraged them to turn it over, but the position of Revolution 9 on the fourth side of the 'White Album' seems designed to deter anyone with normal musical tolerances from getting to the end of the LP. No Good Night for them. Or perhaps that's the intention? Revolution 9 tunes us in, turns us on, turns us off again, tunes us out — the perfect preparation for entering the lost world of this final song.

Fifty years later it's hard to remember that this forgotten realm was the one in which all the musicians of the 1960s British pop scene grew up. Between 1946 and 1967, the only broadcast music available in the UK came from one of the three BBC stations: occasionally the Home Service, but mostly the Light Programme for popular music and the Third Programme for classical music. Even Keith Richards, whom one might imagine had been steeped in the blues from birth, was instead raised on a diet in which chart hits rubbed shoulders with novelty records, songs from the shows and light classical music. As he says in his account of his *Life*: 'we didn't have a record player for a long time, and most of it, for us, was on the radio, mostly on the BBC, my mother being a great twiddler of the knobs […] if there was anything good she'd find it […] including a little bit of Mozart and Bach in the background'.

Of course, the journey into adulthood for Richards, the Beatles and the British musicians of their generation also involved many a trip to the record shop or to friends' houses to hear the latest releases of the new music, especially American music, that the Light Programme never played, and it was by making versions of this music that the Rolling Stones and the Beatles achieved their success. Nevertheless one often has a sense in the British pop of the mid-sixties of a divided musical consciousness — a division between rhythm and blues, rock and roll, and soul, with all their connotations of exciting, liberating, new ideas about sex, class, race and language, and the curiously mixed musical diet of 1950s British radio, switching between Lehar, Vera Lynn, and the Midlands Radio Light Orchestra playing swing. The American music had to be painstakingly learnt, preserving as far as possible the nuances of each musical dialect, whereas the British music was just there, safe in the cupboard of childhood memories, whether good or bad, along with the Bovril and the *Beano*.

Throughout their careers the Beatles would occasionally open this cupboard and make their own versions — either singing covers or composing new songs — of this childhood music. For Lennon and McCartney these shifts in register, crossing the boundary from the music of adolescence back into a prepubescent sound world, usually involve a change in lyrical subject matter too, away from a typically young male obsession with problematic relationships and towards other phases in life, the most famous probably being When I'm Sixty-Four. Good Night makes a similar shift, although in the opposite direction, looking not towards old age but back into early childhood, Ringo tucking us in for the night with a sweet lullaby. It's not the only registral shift on the 'White Album' but its juxtaposition with the avant-garderie of Revolution 9 makes it by far the most shocking.

Ian MacDonald hears the song as 'an inadvertent variation on Cole Porter's True Love, one of the group's old Hamburg standards' but it really isn't. The melodies of True Love and Good Night share a prominent use of the interval of the perfect fourth, and sometimes too their contours are congruent, but there the similarities end. In particular, Good Night lacks the chromatic sophistication of Porter's harmonic language and sticks firmly to the pitches of the D major scale. It is this diatonic simplicity which not only marks the song out as a Lennon rather than McCartney composition but also makes it a pitch-perfect lullaby; if you are lulling a child to sleep, whether you are Brahms writing a Wiegenlied or the author of Twinkle, Twinkle Little Star, stay away from harmonic complexity — it's disturbing.

Almost everything else about the song is pitch-perfect too, just right for bedtime or for a Light Programme broadcast: the string orchestration, the dabbing in of spots of additional instrumental colour from flutes and French horn, even the casting of the Mike Sammes Singers as the accompanying vocal ensemble, because they were the regular backing singers for most Light Programme shows. The one false note is Ringo's lead vocal, yet it is this that lifts the track out of pastiche or parody and into art. Already dressed up in the smooth professionalism of George Martin's arrangement, the careful artlessness of Lennon's song would surely have been unbearably twee if it had been sung by any of the other Beatles.

Did Ringo play up to his role within the Beatles as the Artless Dodger to keep himself in a job, or was this a reflection of who he really was? Whatever the truth, his performance of Good Night is reassuringly unprofessional, although this in turn is part of a British tradition of vocal artlessness which reaches back to George Formby and was represented in the Beatles era by Ken Dodd, whose recording of Tears had topped the UK charts just three years before the release of the 'White Album'. It is also, I suspect, what so bemused American Beatles fans like Jonathan Gould, unable to understand why and how Lennon might write such a song and also unable to hear that while the song may be the musical equivalent of a 'warm tub', Ringo's voice fills it with pathos rather than bathos.

Gould also reports that the *Times* music critic William Mann 'collapsed in laughter' when he heard Good Night. This too is not surprising; classical music establishment figures like Mann wanted to draw the Beatles' songwriting into a classical canon stretching from Schubert to Maxwell Davies, a frame of reference within which George Formby and Ken Dodd are less easily accommodated.

This perhaps takes us to the heart of the Beatles' achievement in the 'White Album'.

By 1968 they were so famous that they felt able to record and release whatever they wanted, so famous that they had reached a point where they were able to engage in a dialogue with their own public image ('here's a clue for you all, the walrus is Paul'). Good Night is then the perfect coda to a Beatles double album whose many imperfections are in the end just another part of its Beatles-ness, a song in which they disappear into their collective past.

Appendix: Off White

DAVID KEREKES

The Beatles missed a trick with the 'White Album' and another possible clue for us all. In the wind-out groove of side four why not the jet plane landing that opens the album? A return to the screeching rubber tyres of touchdown, suggesting that everything before it, sandwiched between touchdowns, is a fractious dream. Maybe an unrealised episode of *The Twilight Zone*, or a forgotten story by Harlan Ellison, or one by Richard Brautigan (an author late to arrive to the cover of *Sgt Pepper*).

While this 'White Album' reprise does not exist, indulge me a moment and 'revisit' it per a 'White Album' bootleg. Thus we might end this book as it started, with a return to the first track on *The Beatles*: Back In The U.S.S.R.

A quick note: Bootlegs are unofficial albums that defy copyright and ownership, manufactured for profit but sometimes fun and almost always by fans.

Beatles bootlegs tend to fall into several broad camps, sometimes a couple of them at once. A bootleg track might be an outtake, an outfake, or an alternate mix of existing tracks, or live material, or unlistenable rubbish for completists only.

Of this unlistenable rubbish for the completist, we can thank the sound effect library at Abbey Road studios. Snippets of audio effects from this library appear on mid- to later years Beatles tracks. The jet plane sound of Back In The U.S.S.R. is a good example, a noise that draws the listener in and helps position the lyric. ('Flew in from Miami Beach B.O.A.C.'...)

Other examples can be found on *Sgt Pepper's Lonely Hearts Club Band*, notably the audience noise of the title track and the cock crow and animal noises of Good Morning Good Morning. Many of these extraneous sounds have been isolated by bootleggers and appear in their entirety on bootlegs such as *The Lost Pepperland Reel And Other Rarities* (Vigotone 1994). (Here the Sgt Pepper crowd noise is track listed as Billy Shears Applause.)

On *Magical Mystery Tour Recording Sessions Reconstructed: Outtakes and Outfakes* (label unknown) one can enjoy, as I do, the coach sound used for the opening track of the Beatles TV movie *Magical Mystery Tour*. In other words, the sound of a coach roaring past.

The Beatles were free to consult and use the Abbey Road sound effects as were other artists working at the studio (Pink Floyd used them a lot). These records had titles like *EMI Sound Effect Record No. 6: Cars*. But there was also magnetic tape of sound effects recorded specifically by the studio toward building a sound effects archive. A number of these reels, maybe all of them, information is scant, were recorded by studio engineer Stuart Eltham. Reel Vol 1 is identified as *General S.F.X.* and contains such things as 'Children audience continuous laughter' plus 'Boxing match. Cheers & whistles. See also Vol 33.' Eltham began travelling the country in the late fifties/early sixties, making these pioneering field recordings using a portable EMI tape machine.

There are sounds from the archive on the 'White Album', although not nearly as many as appear on *Sgt Pepper*. An alternate mix of Back In The U.S.S.R. appears on the bootleg, *The Alternative White Album* (Pear Records, 1998), with longer jet noise at the

beginning and end of the track.

I asked someone who understands music about the jet plane noise and how it works in context of Back In The U.S.S.R. Fellow 'White Album' book contributor Christopher Fox had this to say.

'The screeching works because we know what it is — I don't think there's anything particularly significant about the sound (either timbre or pitch) and it would be quite entertaining to replace it with something else and see if that worked too. It's a very treble-rich sound and the recording is also very lively in the upper frequencies so it merges well with everything else.'

Bootleg albums have great titles. A lot of the Beatles bootlegs have quasi mystical titles, which I suspect is the influence of Krishna Consciousness and the pursuit by Beatles — Harrison in particular — of a more spiritual outlook. *Arrive Without Aging*, *Untouched By the Hand of Madness*, *Gone Tomorrow Here Today*, *Renaissance Minstrels*, *The Beginning & The Middle & Forever*, and so on.

One 'White Album' bootleg, *Off White* (unknown, 1988), is considered by some as a keystone Beatles bootleg. (As of writing it's on Amazon.com, of all places, described as a 'rare test pressing by Hawk Records'.) It contains acoustic working versions of many of the songs that would eventually form the 'White Album', most in this case recorded at home. These recordings give an insight into the Beatles creating what they did, as well as showing that their work during this period was pretty much good to go by the time it reached the studio.

Given its vintage and despite several scarce tracks (mooted as outfakes in some quarters), the quality of *Off White* itself is patchy and has been superseded by several other 'White Album' bootlegs, including *Whiteology* (six volumes) (Walrus Records, 1997), *From Kinfauns To Chaos* (Vigotone, 1999), and *Release from Limitation: The White Album Demos* (Remasters Workshop, 2010).

Back In The U.S.S.R. exists among these demos in a gently played, quietly sung form, almost as if the recording is taking place at night when everyone else in the house is asleep. There is no flashiness to the demo. The matter-of-fact vocal from Paul McCartney crudely double tracked at times, but that's about it for production tics.

McCartney is having fun, even singing a guide for the discordant guitar solos as they would appear in the final cut.

Christopher Fox again, in reference this time to the discordant guitar solos of the final cut.

'Those guitar solos aren't discordant — in the first one George plays the tune! The second one is a typical guitar trick — you hold a high note (technically we'd call this a "high pedal tone") that belongs in one of the chords underneath. Bach does this a lot, although he often has the pedal tone in a middle voice.'

The guitar climb to the chorus? Christopher continues:

'George is just arpeggiating (good technical term) the chord changes, with the top note in each arpeggio a tone higher than the one before.'

The cyclic repetition of music and lyric at 0.57 mins into the song ('Back in the U.S., Back in the U.S., Back in the U.S.S.R.')?

'That sort of repetition is as old as the hills — loop a bit of the line then give us the complete line. Of course, right now I can't think of another example. Wait, "We are Leeds, we are Leeds, we are Leeds United." There's one.'

Back to bootlegs. McCartney's demo of Back In The U.S.S.R., 'unplugged' if you will, is missing the jet plane touchdown that opens the 'White Album'. Lifted from the Abbey Road sound effects archive, the jet plane noise can be found in isolation on bootleg. Except... now that I look for it I can't find it. I'm not able to say much about the track or how long it is because I can't find it. All I can find is older McCartney reminiscing on YouTube about how he made the jet plane noises for Back In The U.S.S.R. Beneath a half-whistle he mimics the sound of a jet plane taking off and a jet plane landing.

McCartney should know. But contrary to what he says on YouTube, the passable half-whistle isn't the noise that furnishes the opening track on the 'White Album'. It's moot anyway. The noise I'm looking for, the jet plane noise, unlistenable rubbish for completists only, I can't find. In the end it must remain absent from the close of this book and my intended fantasy 'White Album' reprise.

Contributors

BLUE-JOHN BENJAMIN is a singer and writer. <bluejohnbenjamin.com>

SAM CAMERON is an economist. He is co-editor of the *Journal of Cultural Economics* and author of *Music in the Marketplace — A Social Economics Approach*. He has also recently edited the first ever reference work collection of articles on the Economics of Music (over 700 pages). As a child he had the privilege of sleeping under a Beatles candlewick bedspread bought by a relative.

K.J.DONNELLY is Professor of Film at the University of Southampton. He is author of *Magical Musical Tour* (2016), *Occult Aesthetics: Synchronization in Sound Cinema* (2014), *British Film Music and Film Musicals* (2007), *The Spectre of Sound* (2005) and *Pop Music in British Cinema* (2001). He has edited a number of books on a range of subjects from silent film music to video game music.

JEREMY DYSON is a filmmaker, author and writer for film and television.

BOB FISCHER is a writer and BBC Radio presenter.

CHRISTOPHER FOX is a composer and Professor in Music at Brunel University.

STEPHANIE FREMAUX is a lecturer at Birmingham City University. She has published on the Beatles and David Bowie. Her forthcoming book, *The Beatles on Screen*, will be published soon by Bloomsbury Academic. When not listening to the Beatles, she enjoys listening to David Bowie, Led Zeppelin, and Elton John. Stephanie is also an avid drummer.

MARK GOODALL is a Senior Lecturer at the University of Bradford. He is the author of *Gathering of the Tribe: music and heavy conscious creation* and *Sweet and savage: the world through the mondo film lens*. He co-directed and produced the film *Holy Terrors* (2017) and is singer and guitarist in the band Rudolf Rocker.

JAX GRIFFIN is a filmmaker and director of the Drunken Film Festival <https://www.drunkenfilmfest.com/>

MATT JONES is singer, guitarist and songwriter with The Hepburns.

DAVID KANE is a researcher in the Social Research and Evaluation Unit (SREU) at Birmingham City University. SREU work on a wide range of funded projects relating to social exclusion in the community at large. Dave has been fascinated by pop music since discovering his brother's collection of 1960s singles at a tender age: his MPhil investigated how music fans organize online resources devoted to their object of fandom and he is currently investigating aspects of popular music heritage. In his spare time, Dave plays guitar, writes songs and escapes the city on his motorcycle.

TONY KEEN was four years old when the White Album was released, and didn't discover The Beatles until the mid-1970s, thanks to a couple of aunts. He writes, mostly on Greece and Rome, film, comics and science fiction, and teaches. He was once in a lift with Paul McCartney.

DAVID KEREKES is a writer and publisher. The first album he bought with his own money was *Let It Be*.

MIKE KIRKUP is a Senior Lecturer in Media Studies at Teesside University. His research areas include popular music (particularly Bob Dylan and the Beatles), Hitchcock, classical Hollywood Cinema & horror cinema from the 1920s–1970s. He was also drafted in to play emergency piano with The Quarrymen on the stage of St Peter's Church Hall,

Woolton, in July 2007 during the fiftieth anniversary celebrations of John meeting Paul.

MELISSA MAPLES is a musician, writer, and photographer. She earned her Bachelor of Arts degree from Sir Paul McCartney's Liverpool Institute for Performing Arts, where she specialised in critical aural analysis and sound design. She writes on a range of topics related to music, including co-authoring *The Daily Book of Classical Music*. She is based on the Turkish Riviera, and is currently dividing her time between photography projects, travelling, and learning to play the ukulele.

RICHARD MILLS is a Senior Lecturer in Irish Literature and Popular Culture at St Mary's University, London. He has been programme director for the Film and Popular Culture, Cultural Studies and Irish Studies degrees. He has published extensively on popular music, Irish literature and culture, film, fashion and British television.

BECCY OWEN is a Welsh singer, songwriter, composer, playwright and performer based in Newcastle upon Tyne. The first show she was ever in was at age eight in 1986 and it was a celebration of the Beatles and their music.

DAVID OWEN is a designer, artist and folklorist. He has designed record sleeves for Jim Moray, Eliza Carthy, Jackie Oates and Emily Portman and describes himself as a 'one man advertising agency for folk music'. He was singer/guitarist with The Hollow Men.

JAMES RILEY is Fellow and College Lecturer in English at Girton College, University of Cambridge. He writes on modern and contemporary literature and is currently working on a book about William Burroughs. He blogs at <www.residual-noise.blogspot.co.uk>

PATRICK SEVC's Beatles research has spanned twenty-five years. He was not only drawn to them by their music, but also by the sense of mystique about them, the uncanny feeling that there's much more beneath the surface; the 'Paul is dead' motif being the ultimate rabbit hole to the other side of the Beatles universe.

STEVE SHELLEY is drummer with Sonic Youth.

STEVE SHEPHERD is a music historian, specialising in 20th century British and American popular culture. He ran record shops and a record label and was a music librarian for fifteen years at Manchester's Henry Watson Music Library. Now based in

Paris, he regularly contributes to music publications and works as a freelance manager and booking agent.

JUSTIN SMITH is Professor of Cinema and Television History at the Leicester Media School. He is Reviews Editor for the *Journal of British Cinema and Television* and is Principal Investigator for the Fifty Years of British Music Video project.

CORY STRAND is a drone/noise composer from the United States. Owner of the obscure HNW/drone label Altar Of Waste, Cory also plays guitar in Minneapolis, MN-based bleak shoegaze band Dreamless. He holds degrees in philosophy and cinematography and plans to begin Masters studies in film soon.

DAVID E.WILLIAMS has released numerous recordings of his demented chamber pop for nearly three decades now, but he has also collaborated with other artists on the fringe, including the late goth icon Rozz Williams (Christian Death) and American noise pioneers Deathpile. Currently, Williams plays keyboards in the rising US psych folk band Destroying Angel.

GREG WILSON is a pioneering DJ, record producer and writer whose extensive experience, which stretches back to the mid-seventies, and wide knowledge of popular culture has positioned him as a bridge-builder; making links between the past and present whilst adding new relevance and context in the process.

A HEADPRESS BOOK
First published by Headpress in 2018

[e] headoffice@headpress.com

THE BEATLES
Or, the 'White Album'

Concept and compilation: Mark Goodall
Text and art copyright © respective contributors
This volume copyright © Headpress 2018
Book design: Mark Critchell <mark.critchell@googlemail.com>

The moral rights of the authors have been asserted.

A CIP catalogue record for this book is available from the British Library

ISBN 978-1-909394-60-5 (paperback)
ISBN 978-1-909394-61-2 (ebook)

Headpress. B**k publisher. Pop and Unpop Culture.

Exclusive NO-ISBN special edition hardbacks and other items of interest are available at HEADPRESS.COM